Who is Sambo?

A Journey of Lessons

Stephen Mackey

RoseDog Books

PITTSBURGH, PENNSYLVANIA 15222

The contents of this work including, but not limited to, the accuracy of events, people, and places depicted; opinions expressed; permission to use previously published materials included; and any advice given or actions advocated are solely the responsibility of the author, who assumes all liability for said work and indemnifies the publisher against any claims stemming from publication of the work.

ISBN: 978-0-8059-8631-0
Printed in the United States of America

First Printing

For more information or to order additional books,
please contact:
RoseDog Books
701 Smithfield Street
Third Floor
Pittsburgh, Pennsylvania 15222
U.S.A.
1-800-834-1803
www.rosedogbookstore.com

DEDICATIONS

This book is dedicated to the ONE source of all things. The ONE that expresses its identity in the many - for it is the many that make up the ONE.

To my ancestors, especially my father Fletcher and Grandmother Pauline – There is no me without you, There is no you without me. I am spirit of your Spirit; Blood of your Blood; Bone of your Bone and Flesh of your Flesh. I pray the circle never be broken.

To those Africans taken from their homes, communities and societies and forced to build new ones in a strange land. With all my humbleness I am proud to tell part of your story.

And to my Godfather Oluwo Afolabi A. Epega – thanks for the tool.

ACKNOWLEDGMENTS

Thanks to…

…the Osun Angels who brought me blessings. I could not have completed it without you.

…Sandy, for your help on re-starting and giving your special energy to the project.

…Velika Johnson-Hines and Warriors of Truth for your support.

…Sheila Savannah for your creative pencil.

…Tracy Beavers on your last minute heroics – we ain't done!

Special thanks to Mother Vivian; my brothers; sisters; and four sons.

And to all my students – clients and God children of my Institute, One Love!

CONTENTS

FOREWORD FROM THE AUTHOR

In writing this book, I wanted to bring something that would not just be out of a need to further expose the injustices and horrors that have occurred in African American ancestry during chattel slavery, but to offer a new awareness of brother and sisterhood by removing certain labels. I pray, this book gives an opportunity for Afrikans, African Americans and others to view the conscious and unconscious self-hate African Americans struggle with and must overcome in order to go forward.

This book is intended to reveal some of the various diversities; social stereotypes; generalizations, and negative attitudes African Americans have towards one another. Moreover, these methods must be understood so that we may stop the myths that lead to our social ills. The core of this story lets us revisit and understand the genesis of self-hate that harbors deep within our minds and behaviors. I describe self-hate best, from the perspective of the character Sambo. Sambo, an African, is the principle hand on the plantation in Harriet Beecher Stowe's classic story <u>Uncle Tom's Cabin</u>. The heartless master of the plantation, Simon Legree, specially trained Sambo to be skilled in savageness, brutality, and cruelty towards all slaves. Systematically, he had been voided of spirit, morality and awareness of self through conditioning. Hence, in hating himself, he hated anything that looked like himself.

Sambo was conditioned to hate Africans, and rightfully so Africans hated him. He always referred to them as niggers. He belittled women and especially hated Tom. Sambo's dislike for Tom stemmed from Tom's work ethic on another plantation, which privileged Tom being first in charge over the slaves whenever Simon went away. Sambo resented Tom, for he knew this responsibility established a closer relationship with the Massa. Simon knew what he was doing because he knew Tom was a spiritually strong individual with moral and respect for his people. Thus by placing him temporarily in charge would somewhat compromise Tom's position with the slaves.

We are now living in the 21st century. A lot has changed and a lot has not. It is no doubt that the spirit of Sambo lives in some African Americans. What we must first understand is that this is a new and improved Sambo. One who often works against his people and community; who sits with authority; one who can create and dictate change but chooses not too; who deals drugs, sells dreams and death and false salvation to his people! This new Sambo is one who is well trained in the best universities, yet poorly educated of self. One who is a dangerous threat because he has planted a future and laid a course that is uncertain. One who is the worst kind of African American as he cares NOT to know his history. Every culture has value and worth, yet the new Sambo chooses to go to the table without his own. This Sambo believes he is a player because he has accepted the ways and beliefs of others.

Information is powerful and it is a concept that has escaped us. It is the one thing in American that continues to hold us back. We do not seek information from the genesis of institutions we give reverence, our time, our money and our energy. It is time we stop and think. It is not enough to just accept and believe. Do not give another tithe until the reverend can answer the whys, until the school board can answer the whys, and let the politician not receive another vote until he/she can explain the whys! Quit signing those contracts to rap, sing and act in those arena's that are degrading to yourself and Black people.

We must teach to have respect for our communities and ourselves. We have bought into other cultures, traditions and holidays though we may not even know or understand the history. We say," That's the way it's been done for years; Yeah its tradition!"

Although we have Kwanzaa most African Americans do not celebrate it because they feel it is anti-Christian. Now that's amazing. If the Irish can designate a day of remembrance to pay homage to their ancestors and witness Halloween and St. Patrick's Day grow to nationally celebrated holidays, not to mention to watch the Mexican Americans celebrate the Day of the Dead; then can we at last have a day that recognizes the millions of African Americans that were victims of our Holocaust?

To reconnect back is the definition of the word religion. We as African Americans need to reconnect back to the spiritual consciousness of ourselves. Out of this spirituality is born the ideas that give people the motivation to produce and maintain for themselves. We must continue to keep assessing the information that is consistent with our history and traditions. We then have to manifest it into the mainstream of our communities, institutions of education, politics, religion and economics.

We have so much more than our slave ancestors could imagine. We possess every opportunity to reach back and get what was once ours; what our ancestors had taken away from them on every slave auction block on which they stood.

We could never imagine the rich culture, spirituality and heritage that was stripped from them.

We must strengthen our own institutions so that we learn to have the respect and admiration for our communities and ourselves. The European has respect for his community and religion. We see this respect on television, and even in "our" schools and churches, as well as Arabs. Hispanics are respected because they have their name and homeland, Asians for their culture and homeland, and Jews due to their remembrance of their holocaust saying "never again" and creating museums. Italians, Irish and French practice ways of the "old country," and even Native Americans, who even in colonization, paid homage to their ancestors and still do so today with rituals and sacred times and season. African Americans…well, let's see; we practice and celebrate others cultures; we do not have strong communities, corporations or financial institutions. We lack respect for our native country or ancestors. Repeatedly, we not only make fun of Africa, some of us celebrate the fact that being brought here was the "good thing" that came out of slavery. So I guess if anyone did respect us, it would be, because we are basically trying to emulate them. Think so…of course not. What nationality or culture of people in this country has packed their hair with hot combs and chemicals to favor Africans? What group gets plastic surgery to have a broader nose? How many athletic celebrities of other races marry or even date Black people?

This conditioning or programmed behavior that I call self-hate is actually none other than a lack of knowledge of ourselves as a people and most importantly a lack of self-awareness and self-love as a person.

We cannot save ourselves by denying our history and who we are as a person or people; or by being "afro centric." We cannot think that the first Black president can save our communities; or Oprah must donate all her time and assets to Black causes and call her and others of her status "sellouts."

So dear Brothers and Sisters, ask yourselves... Who am I? Where do I come from? Why did this happen to my people; and where do I go from here? Please, do not let the Bible be your only source of information, but pray with all sincerity...and the answers to your questions will come.

"The Great Maafa or Great Destruction for the African American."

If you went to the GA Adangbe people of West Africa Ghana Region, they will tell you that we are the Canaanites, they make no bones about it. They are explicit about who they are. They have ceremonies and celebrations to remember those days when they were in the Land of Canaan before having been driven out by invaders. And they tell a story of how they migrated down the Peninsula by the Red Sea we call Saudi Arabia, and how they go into Yemen, and how they crossed over into Ethiopia, how they dwelled in Ethiopia, how they moved into the Chad Basin and Boreneo and how they finally ended up having come through Nigeria and Benin and they ended up on the Accra Plains where they found peace for themselves again.

If you go to any of the major people in Africa they will tell you a story of migration before the Atlantic Slave trade, of the forced migrations by invasions from the North. They will tell you how they were uprooted and had to take their institutions in their minds as philosophical perspective because they could not carry the buildings with them.

And so here we are in North America telling a story that nobody wants to hear and sometimes we do not want to hear our own story. A story about these African American people who possess or seemingly in Possession of 160 plus

educational institutions of higher learning and won't even teach our own history, and don't even seriously reflect on our own culture. WE go to institutions we call churches, Mosques and synagogues but don't want to know the genesis of these institutions for fear you may see a reflection in the mirror of yourself and I wonder if that fear is the fact that it will put responsibilities on your that you don't want
Dr. James Smalls (Speaks)
Professor City College of New York.
12/95 – Houston, Texas/ Shrine of the Black Madonna Culture Center and Bookstore

Chapter I

VOICES FROM THE FIELD

I have been called many names throughout my life. There are a few I don't care to remember. Horus Williams is the name I was given sixty years ago. The last of those thirty years I've come to be known throughout the community as the resident field slave. My work and editorials at the Nubian News, an African community newspaper that is published throughout Texas, has earned me this name in the grassroots community.

Our city, Buffalo Hill, is famous for the bayou it has been built around as it flows through the city; it serves as a dividing line between both races and economic classes. The Southside is predominately black. There are a few middle-class blacks living in the area but most are lower middle-class. All classes of white and a handful of upper-class blacks represent the Northside. Just as popular as the bayou and the bridge that crosses over it, is the midtown of Buffalo Hill, a historically rich area that was built on the north banks of the bayou. Midtown is an area that resembles something out of an old southern plantation picture book, i.e., big pecan trees and lots of manicured green shrubbery. It is called "Augustus Hill," named after the founder of Buffalo Hill, Augustus Peterson. Buffalo Hill could have been easily called Petersonville. The Peterson's are considered the first family in our area and for nearly two hundred years they still maintain that title. The historians say that in 1803, when Augustus

Peterson arrived with his wife and two sons he single-handedly fought off twenty wild Indians. After he drove them away from their village on the bayou, he removed the head of a buffalo from the top of a totem pole standing on a makeshift mound in the center of their village. There he claimed victory and named the village "Buffalo Hill."

On Saturday morning, I drove over to interview an old friend on the Southside of Buffalo Hill. As I approached the bridge, I looked to my right and in a distance I could see the barriers and tape that roped off the area where a theater was going to be built. This was my reason behind coming to talk to my friend.

As I crossed the bridge to reach the heart of the Southside, I rolled down my window and slowed down to about twenty miles an hour. The autumn breeze felt nice as I listened to the rustling of leaves and watched the pecan trees sway from side to side. The folks in the hood had already begun their Saturday morning rituals of front porch conversations. A few old men had gathered under a giant pecan tree for an early game of dominoes. I honked my horn and waved. I then pointed my finger and yelled out to them, "I'll be back!" Smiling and waving as I drove along, I began to think about my friend John Washington. All of his friends called him Rasidi or Ra, a West African name that meant "one who gives good council." I met John about five years ago during an interview at the Nubian. He had recently resigned from Peterson Industries and was at the center of a controversy surrounding a project on the history of the Peterson family and Buffalo Hill. Since that interview he has remained my friend. Whether organizing an event at the neighborhood community center where he worked or rallying to protest an injustice, John was clearly the lifeline of the Southside. Although many had great admiration for him - the majority north of the bayou did not, blacks included. He was a disappointment to them. He was called "Mr. Trouble," by most. Honestly, he was the complete opposite.

John was born and raised in Buffalo Hill and graduated from the local high school. He went to college on a four-year basketball scholarship at Buffalo Hill University. And after his four-year eligibility ended he went to Europe to play in the professional league. He played for one year before returning to Buffalo Hill. John had earned his degree in Sociology during the summer of 1988. Upon graduation he was immediately hired by Peterson Industries to work in their new public relations department. Life went well for the first five years; he received numerous bonuses, raises, was promoted twice and admired by all the big whigs in the company. He was invited to the company's many country club functions and was a standout in the community. John was a very special and unique person. He lived in an upscale townhouse in Augustus Hills, where he attended church and dined in the homes of CEO's and directors of the company. He helped organize blood drives, walk-a-thons, various sport tournaments, and was admired by almost every worker. The blacks that didn't like him thought he was an Uncle Tom and Whites thought he was an uppity nigger, but that didn't bother John.

He was the fifth of six children. His mother and grandmother raised him since his father died when he was four years old. His mother never let him forget who he was as a person over time he became disenchanted with the corporate life. His mother knew this and she constantly reminded him where he came from and told him never to forget his history because if he did forget it would be hard to find his way back. It's not that she was not proud of her son, she was. She told him that his connection to his community was spiritual and must never be broken.

The transformation began when Bob Peterson gave John a project to research. John and four other employees from the human resources and public relations department would complete the task. Bob was not only President and CEO of Peterson Industries, but also represented past generations of Petersons. His request for the group was to trace his family legacy for a portfolio that would be presented to honor the founding father of Buffalo Hill. John spearheaded the group that had an unlimited budget and often stayed out of the office. The group spent many countless hours of researching history at night; at the library and weekends were spent on the computers. Their research first led them to New Orleans and then to the Smithsonian Institute archives in Washington D.C. There they discovered the unimaginable. An official at the Smithsonian confirmed that the Peterson mansion and property was once a slave plantation. He told us how old man Augustus Peterson was one of the largest owners of slaves in the Southwest. The root of his wealth was from the backs and blood of Africans free labor. Records indicated that he started with six slaves and ended up with more than seventy. They revealed the exact dates and timelines of the purchase of slaves at a Galveston auction block. Everything that John had heard from his mother and grandmother was true. He became emotionally devastated.

As he gathered the information the group insisted it was not appropriate to divulge their findings to the community. "You're not thinking clearly. This was something that happened a long time ago," they said, while trying to convince John that he had a commitment to Peterson Industries and that they weren't going to lose their jobs by exposing this dirty little secret. John paid no attention. He just said, "The truth must be known."

After they returned from D.C., Bob Peterson called John into his office and told him he knew everything and the information he discovered was false. Bob said they would put together a new portfolio and the other facts would be set aside. He also told John if he had any thought of releasing the information he would be fired immediately. John told Bob, "So let it be done." The only newspaper that carried the story was the Nubian, written by yours truly.

John tried to retrieve copies of the information from Washington D.C. but was told the records did not exist. The official with whom he had spoken with had an abrupt loss of memory.

John sold his townhouse, gathered all his savings and assets, and moved back home. He took a year off to research what he knew and learned the whole story of the Peterson family. John still couldn't enlist anyone to believe him. Only a few blacks on the Southside and this old-field slave were interested in knowing the truth.

He read book after book of African American history: "Histories of the Slave Trade," "African World History," "Africans in the Bible," "Africans Before the Bible," and "History of the Nile Valley Civilizations." He became a walking encyclopedia of African and African-American culture and history.

So there he was Mr. Trouble, only because he knew the truth and the truth had set him free from the Sambo's of the African community. He used this term quite often to describe Africans who he had perceived to have negative influences on the rest of us. John's desire not to mix with any blacks who were not as conscious about history and society as he, was his only drawback. So he called them "Sambos."

You see Sambo was an overseer on the plantation in Harriet Beecher Stowe's novel, "Uncle Tom's Cabin." Sambo was trained to be cruel towards all slaves by the heartless master of the plantation Simon Legree. Systematically, void of spirit and morality, Sambo's actions reflected the thinking of Simon on how to run a successful plantation. Sambo was taught to hate all Africans; and all Africans hated him because he was close to the massa. He was an African who was skilled in savageness and brutality. He always referred to them as niggers, belittled women, and despised Tom. He felt this way because Simon had told him how good Tom had been on another plantation and that he would be the first in charge whenever Simon went into town or on a trip (Ex: Age-old strategy of divide and conquer). Knowing this would put Tom closer to the massa which made Sambo increasingly resentful of Tom.

From the first day of Tom's arrival, Simon waged an evil war against him to break his spirit using Sambo as a strong-arm against the new slave. To teach Tom a lesson, Sambo was instructed to whip him after Tom refused to whip a female slave. As Tom takes his punishment, he asserts his faith in God much to the resentment of Simon. This makes the plantation master even angrier. Simon then orders Sambo to take every drop of blood Tom had in his body. This delighted Sambo to the utmost, but Tom continued to praise God calling His name until his last breath. In a surprising act of mercy, Sambo attempted to call Tom back to consciousness because he was so moved by his spiritual strength. Unfortunately, it was too late; as Tom died, Sambo cried endlessly.

The scenario is a classic metaphor of physical and spiritual freedom. Sambo accepts freedom of the body and Tom accepts freedom of the spirit. This is how most Africans' fate is measured. Our lifestyle, jobs and our interpretations of western society shows a willingness to accept the ways of others; the end results have not served us as well as expected. Such as the way we raise our children today.

If I had never studied "Uncle Tom's Cabin," I would likely continue to view Tom as most African-Americans do; a spineless sellout that has no connection to his people and their culture and who lacks respect for the struggles of his ancestors on whose backs he stands. Tom was a hero in this story, Sambo the sellout.

So John told me to ask myself, "What is the difference between the fictional Sambo and today's socially-created African-Americans? Who is the co-conspirator of the assassination of the African spirit? Who is Sambo?"

John explained to me that even though we are living in the 21st century much had not changed. There is no doubt that the spirit of Sambo lives in some Africans. What we must first understand is that this spirit is a new and improved Sambo, one who often works against his people and community without direct contact. One who sits with authority, deals drugs, sells dreams and death to his people; one who is well trained in the best universities - but poorly educated. One who is often looked upon by unconscious people, but has no real respect for them. One who is a dangerous threat because he has planted a future and laid a course that is uncertain and spiritually unclean; one who is the worst kind of African because he cares not to know his history John says, "Be conscious and aware."

I arrived at the two-story duplex where my friend lived and got out of my car. I waved at a few of the elders cheerfully and headed up the stairs to John's apartment. Halfway up I could hear the resounding words of a passionate Malcom X coming from an audiocassette. "Before you were a Democrat or a Republican you were Black. Before you were a Christian or Muslim you were Black. Before you were an

American and caught hell you were Black," said Malcom.

As I reached the top of the stairs, I noticed the door to John's apartment was opened. John was sitting in a rocking chair with his head nodding slowly back and forth. The words from the tape were the very essence of his state of liberation. I dared to interrupt but was anxious to hear his story on what's been eating at the heart of this town.

I yelled out over the tape "Hey! Hey!" John turned his head towards me flashed his patented smile and stood up. John is a tall and slender man and stood six feet four inches with well-defined muscles and brown skin. He wore natural locs, a sacred hairstyle, which popped out of his head resembling that of a free man who has felt no need for styling. The most distinguished thing about him was his eyes. They were strong, kind, and dark seeming to smile and give off some sort of aura of wisdom.

We walked toward each other grinning, laughing, shaking hands, and hugging. As we both stepped back my friend could not help but poke at my mid-section.

"Man! Those are some serious love handles. Is it good living or just pork?" asked John.

I couldn't help but laugh at what he had asked, so I said, "A lot of both!"

He gestured with his hand for me to take a seat offering me a cup of his famous coffee. I took him up on his offer. As I watched my friend walk into the kitchen, arms swaying in a rhythmic motion, I thought how intimidating this brother could be at times. I guess he felt he had to.

He yelled out to me "cream and sugar?"

"Yes Sir! I'm not use to imported Kenyan coffee."

I made a quick survey of his apartment. The African artifacts on the mantel were beautiful. Most of them were of the West African Orisha's of the Ifa spiritual system that some of our ancestors were practicing before Christianity and Islam was forced upon them during enslavement. He had several woodcarvings of animals, warriors, kings and queens. He had a few paintings of ancient Egyptian figures that hung behind a black leather sofa. On the other side of the room were a homemade office with a desk, computer, printer, fax machine, copier and a shelf with numerous books on history. Behind all of that was a map of the world serving as wallpaper. What stood out more than anything was the beautiful rug in the middle of the room; it was a Kente print in blends of various colors.

John put down my cup, "So you wanna know what really happened huh?"

"I wouldn't want anything else but the truth my friend. That's why I'm here."

He looked at me very seriously. I knew what I was about to hear was none other than the truth.

"What I am about to tell you Horus is more than just truth. It goes beyond anything you could ever imagine."

I knew John was serious. I grabbed my briefcase. "Mind if I tape all of this?" "No, but you might wanna make sure you got enough tape."

I put the tape recorder on the table that lay between us. John took a sip of his coffee, as did I. I stared at him with eagerness and anticipation; he lowered his head and then looked at the window where the rays of sun fought their way through the Venetian blinds and sipped with pleasure the fresh ground Kenyan coffee. He realized that the dawn of a new day had already taken place.

"It was spiritual Horus.

He rose slowly from his chair and stood. He put down his coffee cup and started toward the window. There was silence for a moment. I turned on the tape to record.

"Ready whenever you are friend."

John began.

I stood right here at this window about this time last week. I opened the blinds to see the new day, but I couldn't believe what was before my eyes. There on a branch on the weeping willow tree sat a magnificent looking bird. I marveled in awe at the feathers that blended so evenly and smoothly into one another the sharp and piercing eyes, the lean legs, the design of the claws and the talons of death draped over the branch. I stood there looking at this wonder of nature. The bird's head and neck moved with the blink of an eye from side to side, I said to myself. "Today is the day that I must stand on my ancestors and not let them be forgotten in today's madness." I pledged to be a predator and not the prey of an injustice. At that moment the bird turned toward me and we made eye contact. The spirit of the stare gave me approval for my promise. I was struck by the look of the bird and I knew I wouldn't fail. It let out a loud screech and sprang from the branch with its wings spread wide. It majestically headed toward the blinding rays of the sun. I quickly opened the blinds all the way desperately trying to look at this beautiful creature, but it was too late.

I faced the playing tape where the words of Malcom still rang out and marveled at how they fit the moment of my encounter with the bird. I turned the tape off and began to prepare for the day ahead believing it would be special.

I put in a CD an African chant and started to dress. After I finished I gave a libation to the ancestors.

"What's a libation John?"

"It's an acknowledgment to give and receive blessings from our ancestors."

"There're a few ways to conduct it but I'll explain what I did that morning."

I proceeded to explain, "I walked over to the glass coffee table removed the hand crafted ornaments on it and reached down under the table for a box. I removed a bottle of alcohol and a cloth. I poured some of the alcohol into the cloth and wiped the glass, cleaning it thoroughly. I unfolded and placed a white sheet over the table listening to the drums from the song that played. I then took a plant off the kitchen table, a beautiful African violet, sat it on the table and brought out a bottle of spring water. I dropped to my knees with my palms at waist length looked up to God and spoke. 'Almighty Creator the intelligence within, I thank thee for the strength of my ancestors who came before me.'"

"I then poured water into the plant. I repeated the word Ashe (A-shay), which reflects "Amen" and poured water into the soil of the flowerpot after each saying to confirm my honesty respect and sincerity to the universe and the divine forces."

"I thank thee for my ancestors may their spiritual power guide me Ashe! I thank thee for my parents through whom you brought me here, Ashe! I thank thee for giving me the breath of life on this day, Ashe! I am calling for help from the Orisha's, they must give me strength."

"I stood up and walked over to that picture there, Horus and I asked the brother to give me strength. As I got a closer look at the portrait of the man to whom John was referring to, I noticed it was the face of a man with dark skin and dark steel-like eyes. His hair was naturally uneven the lips full the nose broad and he was looking up to the heavens." The portrait read at the bottom "The Spiritual Revolutionary Messiah." I turned to John, "That's a powerful message."

He replied, "There is one bigger than that in the story I am about to tell you."

I sat back down. John went to get us a refill bringing back the whole pot. I guess this was to signal to me that I would be giving my full attention to hear what he had to tell. He began again.

As I went downstairs and smelled the new day I glanced at my watch. The time was ten o'clock. I looked at the people who were out and about feeling the pulse of the community on a beautiful day in Buffalo Hill the pride of South Texas. Summer and its heat and humidity had passed. It was now mid-October the fall season or Indian summer the shortest season in this bayou city. Before I walked across the street a middle-aged man pushing a shopping cart greeted me. He is a Vietnam veteran nicknamed G.I. Joe who had elected himself as the neighborhood watchdog. He smiled with only a few teeth in his mouth his oily skin shining blissfully from the sun.

"Wha ya say my brudder! You up mite late this mawning. Pardy pardy all night."

I replied, "Ain't no partying go be gon on without you G.I. Joe." I laughed and gave Joe two dollars and asked him to keep an eye on my place for the day.

"No problem brudder," said Joe.

I started across the street when the horn blew from an oncoming car. It was a brand new shiny red Mustang convertible. The car had aluminum alloy rims and the sunrays that were bouncing off them were blinding. The music was thumping so loudly the vibration was felt in the street. The car slowly came to a stop and the power windows slid down.

"Whazz up tall dark and handsome?" said the woman.

She leaned out of the window checking me out from feet to head.

"Are you coming to the ceremony today?" she asked.

I smiled. "Hello Katherine. Yeah I'll be there. Hi ya doing?"

Katherine answered, "Fine just like you and you don't haft to call me Katherine." My name is "Couchi." You can just say Kat like everyone else. Have you bought my CD?"

"No but I am working on it," I said.

She looked at me and said, "Huh! Yeah right. But I ain't mad atcha. When we gon hook up? You too much man to be alone in that apartment." She playfully popped the chewing gum in her mouth.

I said, "You know we won't hook up. I know your whole family and I ain't going out like that. Besides after watching you grow up in the hood and church I'm still mad at you for making that CD with that ol' Sambo Aaron or whatever y'all call him."

"Black Dawg," she said, upset at me as though this was a parent-child relationship.

I told her, "Kat you know what? I know you understand the difference between clean and dirty. Baby you are beautiful with that caramel skin and your soft brown eyes. Your natural hair and smile can light up a room."

She sat mesmerized and replied shyly, "Oh Ra. You so crazy!"

I continued raising my voice a little. "Now you got that blond hair, blue contacts, a gold tooth in your mouth, and a pound of makeup. You got tattoos and you half-naked. Girl you got two kids! You really need to look at yourself."

Kat stopped smiling and said, "O.K.! Fo yo info-mation, this blond haired, blue-eyed, tattooed, and gold tooth stuff you talkin about fo yo info-ma-tion has got me a record contract half-naked or not Mr. Black Man!"

I said, with a smile, "I love you too."

Kat grew even angrier, and with one move hit the gas pedal and sped off. I jumped back quickly and waved at her still smiling.

I continued across the street and went to a neighbor's house. I knocked on the door and entered. The smell of incense filled the air. African art and artifacts along with whatnots and scriptures decorated the walls. It looked like a museum. On the mantel were pictures that the homeowner had taken with Martin Luther King, Malcom X, Kwame Ture (Stokley Carmichael), Angela Davis, Jesse Jackson, and Louis Farrakhan. There were degrees in history, philosophy, and sociology from Grambling, Prairie View, and Texas Southern and a honorary degrees from Spellman were displayed.

This was the home of the wisest and most intelligent person I knew, Mrs. Imani Ashante. She was also a root woman from the Gullah Islands off the coast of South Carolina. These islands are well known for their African cultural traditions. Miss Imani is a Yoruba priestess well taught in spirituality. Her ancestors settled in the islands and she was raised there in Yoruba traditions. After her husband mysteriously died at the hands of the police she moved here with her two children. Miss Imani once told me that her ancestral mother was from Buffalo Hill and that her spirit had guided her here. I believed her. She possessed the kind of wisdom that would pick someone apart and then put them back together again. Everything she talked about was in alignment with one's spiritually. She believed God was in all things, at all times.

I walked over to the table where the lady sat. The table was decorated with an African Kente print, blue and black with a touch of sun gold, a basket of fruit, a small freshly baked cake and three lit white candles. She said, very slowly and authoritatively, "You are late!"

I looked at my watch. "It's only five minutes Miss Imani," I humbly said. She looked at me sternly. "Five minutes can get you a mile head start when you are being chased."

"I most humbly apologize Miss Imani."

"It's okay. Now lets get down to business."

The table had been prepared for an offering to the ancestors of Buffalo Hill, and to receive what Miss Imani called the voices from the field. She proceeded with the prayer reaching over the table with outstretched arms and motioning with her fingers for me to place my hands on hers. I did so gently and slowly but as she grabbed them I felt a strong pulse flow though my body. It was a dull strong pain. My heart began to beat faster. I could barely open my eyes and as I looked across the table I saw the bottom of her chin and the white African cower shells that surrounded her neck. Her head was hung all the way back. She then flung her head forward the locs on her head now draped across the table like wild vines in a dense forest. My pain faded as she squeezed my hand tighter. I felt a cold haunting sensation and began to breathe heavily and pant rapidly. Various images were taking over my thoughts and consciousness. I saw things from long ago; fields, old ships, and I began to hear cries from babies and women. I heard shouts by men in a strange language. I saw white men in hats riding horses and a naked black man running. I heard a voice of a woman saying, "Go back and come again!"

I folded my eyebrows in confusion and a woman appeared. She had dark eyes and bloodstains were on her face.

"I give you our blood," she said.

I gave out a low shout of fear and disbelief and my head fell down nearly hitting the table. I returned to consciousness and raised my head. Miss Imani was staring at me with a frightened look.

I asked, "What happened?"

She hesitated to answer.

"Huh?" I asked.

Miss Imani then said slowly, "You have seen a vision of the past; all your knowledge of our people will now come to judgment. Do you know the season according to the stars ?"

"Yes, it is the time of the scorpion where certain periodical winds bring vapors burning like the venom of the scorpion or storms." Known to Westerners as the hurricane season.

"Good!" she replied and then continued. "The ancestors have told me that the scorpion will bring the Ka to the ceremony at the highest time of the sun."

"The Ka?" I yelled.

"Yes the Ka! Do you know what it is?"

I said, "Yea The Ka in ancient Kemetic (Egyptian) civilization was the vital energy which both sustained and created life. Funerary rites were spoken to the Ka of the deceased."

"Good!" she said. "Now it is time. What you know will save you. Don't let their attitudes of today destroy them."

"Save who? Whose attitudes? Miss Imani what are you talking about?"

"Go now to the ceremony," she said.

I was puzzled and confused but I knew that somehow it had to make sense. I stood and turned for the door. Miss Imani rose and walked slowly behind me. I turned around to face her.

"They must all know why it is they exist," she said.

"So what you are saying, is that a strong wind like the Scorpion will bring energy for the transformation of the Ka at noon today?" I asked.

She looked at me and said, "Nothing."

"Yeah okay Miss Imani." I hugged her then kissed her on the forehead.

"You are never alone my child never alone," she said.

I crossed the street stepped into my car and drove away.

While the cool breeze of the fall season blew into the car, I sang with a low tone to Marvin Gaye's, "What's Going On" coming from my rear speakers. 'But who are they to judge us just because our hair is long.' I moved my head rhythmically to the sound rolling through the hood at about twenty-five miles an hour waving and blowing my horn at a friend. I was still confused about what took place with the bird and then at Miss Imani's.

I contemplated the ceremony Kat had spoken of wondering how it could even occur - the ground breaking of a new movie theater being built on the site of an old cemetery. Many, myself included, believed this was a slave cemetery. This ground breaking was being done in an area on the north edge of the bayou also known as "Freedmen's Town." I firmly believed many of us, still living here, are descendants of slaves that worked the fields of Buffalo Hill.

The area had become a victim of gentrification. The revitalization of downtown nightlife that resembled other major cities was very appealing and had already been deemed inevitable. A few others and I considered this area the last frontier in an ongoing battle with the city and fat land developer Peterson Industries. Many of us with grassroots organizations were fighting to keep this a black historical area. But, the city's campaign of revitalization seemed much too powerful.

What really chapped me was thinking about who had been enlisted by the sponsor Bob Peterson to support this project and event. They were six local celebrities who were born on the Southside. They had made a name for themselves at the expense of their own community and now resided on the Northside. The idea that they were somehow giving back to the community helped them live up to their name Sambo.

I turned into the neighborhood café "Brenda's," parked my car and walked in. I held my hand up high and motioned to a lady who smiled cheerfully at me.

"Hotep," I said my African greeting of hello.

The lady replied "Hotep my brother. Whacha gon have today?"

"I'd like a veggie burger on wheat with a glass of soy milk to go my sister," I said.

Brenda was the owner and hostess of the cafe. She said, "Um-um is that how you stay so slender and fine man?"

"Well, that's how I stay slender - fine I don't know," I replied.

She yelled my order to the people behind the counter. As I sat down on a barstool, I noticed a gentleman sitting near-by. I quickly looked him over. He was wearing a fine suit, an exquisite watch, two rings and he smelled of designer cologne. I nodded up at him. "Hotep."

The gentlemen said, "Hello," not really knowing how to respond.

Brenda brought the distinguished man a cup of coffee and took his order. The man added cream and sugar to his cup stirring slowly as he wrestled with the challenge of how to speak to me. I was lost watching a T.V. report about the groundbreaking of the new theater. I shook my head in disgust.

Brenda asked, "What time are you going down there, cause I know you're going?"

I looked at her and gave her a smile. "High noon it's going down."

She laughed "Boy you crazy. Now you know those high-dollar folks gonna be there and they don't like you. The cops, the T.V. and radio people gonna be there too, so please be careful. You hear me?"

"Yeah I hear ya," I said.

The gentleman next to me was still trying to figure out how to speak to me. He was checking me out during the conversation with Brenda looking at the locs on my head and the black mock turtleneck with the letters F.O.M.B.A.S. on it.

He blurted out "What does "Hotep" mean?"

I told him it was an East African greeting that meant "peace".

The man was still curious. "What do those letters on your shirt stand for?"

"Freedom of mind body and spirit," I said.

"You are very creative. Did you make the garment yourself?" He responded.

"No," I replied. "I have a friend who makes them. Would you like to buy one?"

"Uh no thanks," he said, "I would have surely guessed that you were the designer."

I questioned, "Why's that?"

"Well," the man said, "you look like a man who is really into his roots or how do you uh.....say uh......culture! Yeah that's it culture."

I shook my head, "Oh yeah?"

The man took a sip of his coffee swirled his barstool around to me and asked

"What is your religion?"

Brenda who had been listening said, "Uh-oh! Clear the room."

The man looked confused. I turned very slowly. My left eyebrow arched as the man looked at me and gulped. "I have graduated from that which you refer to as religion." I said.

"Well where do you attend church?" He added.

"My home. And, by the way, what culture are you off into?"

"I was born in America so I recognize the traditions and holidays of my country," the man answered in a bourgeois tone.

I said, "Okay so where do you live and attend church?"

"Augustus Hills!" The enthusiasm in his voice carried a hint of "How do you like those apples?" He said, "I attend Augustus Hill Community Church," as if it were some big accomplishment.

I again said, "Okay," already instinctively knowing what kind of man he was. He was dressed really sharp and neatly shaven, I really didn't have a problem with it. Hell, I once dressed the same way. But I knew this brother was the kind who liked to talk and rave about what he has and is going to get. He would like everyone to know this about him. That he was the model for the successful black man thinking he had something we all wanted. I continued to ask him questions.

"So where are you from and what university did you attend?"

He eagerly replied, "I'm from inner-city Houston. I attended Westland University, which you know is like the Ivy League. I have two degrees and I work for Peterson Industries so guess you can say I've made it."

"Made it where?" I asked.

"Out of the ghetto," he said.

I stood up slowly. My six feet four inches and broad shoulders towered over the man. I could tell he was slightly intimidated. I looked down at him said, "How long have you had this problem?"

The man looked up at me. "What problem?"

"Well," I said, "You're obviously well trained but you're fighting who you are and where you came from. You feel guilty about your position so you try to win the admiration of the African folk you think you left behind to cover up your guilt. You play golf and you don't like it. You go to that church and you don't want to be there. You see that blond haired blue-eyed Lord on that picture and it doesn't feel right. You listen to other music but it really doesn't make you move, does it? Naw my brother a slave is never satisfied."

The man looked at me angry and confused. He stood up but was still much shorter than I was.

"You don't know a damn thing about me and I'm not your brother! Nigger you don't know nothing!"

I replied, "Then why does a African-American man with your credentials ride through this part of town in an expensive car and walk in here on a Saturday morning? Huh? You sho ain't from around here; You want approval my brother but, you cut your ties and nobody in here can give it back to you...that's why you're here."

Silence filled the room for a few seconds. I had obviously struck a nerve with this gentleman. He looked around at the other customers who were looking at him in shame. I extended my hand to him for a handshake. He slowly looked down at my hand. His face was in shameful disbelief. He was broken by my words. He raised his head and shook my hand.

I smiled and said, "come in here... with sincerity ...Hotep Brother."

I turned to the counter and picked up my order then headed for the door yelling to Brenda, "Peace Out!"

"Be careful," Brenda yelled.

I knew when I left the man was in shock. He had judged me to be a black militant a back-to-Africa uneducated fool. Brenda mentioned to me later on that she had told the man to look on the bright side of the confrontation. He could have spent a lot of money on a shrink and still be screwed up.

I drove out of the neighborhood crossing the bridge to the Northside.

The roads that normally led to the black historical area had been blocked off so I had to take another route. Unfortunately, that route was Augustus Drive the main street that ran right through Augustus Hill. I figured somehow that this was by design, a sort of scenic appetizer, and a realization of the ceremony.

As I passed through this rich area I thought of the name that folks on the Southside had given it - "Up on the Hill." It had earned this name through the years. "Up on the Hill" was where most of our elder kin people worked as maids, butlers, housekeepers, yardmen, and chauffeurs.

"You had some work up there too! Huh Horus?"

"Yes sir. I most surely did. Matter of fact, those roots are what has kept me here all these years," said Horus.

As I drove slowly on Augustus Drive, obeying the twenty-five miles-an-hour speed limit, I thought about the research I had done and the stories I had read about on the history of this area. How the blood, sweat, and long hot backbreaking days of free salve labor helped amassed the wealth of all of this. I looked from side to side at the huge homes, plush landscaped lawns, picturesque statues, cobblestone driveways and pecan trees hanging over the street touching other trees across from them nearly blocking all the sun and its rays.

I arrived at a stop sign at Peterson's Way. The street was named after the city's first family and inhabitants of the big mansion a quarter mile to the left. The designer and builder of the home was Augustus Peterson, so the town's record stated. The records also stated that cattle raising and farming amassed the wealth of this family. But when I researched the records they all had one common thread. They all started in late October 1831 and Buffalo Hill was discovered in 1803. That meant twenty-eight years of history was missing. This is why three co-workers and me went to Washington D. C.. In the archives we discovered of the land commission all the records of a fully operated slave plantation. We found a bill of sales for human cargo, cotton, sugar and corn being transported and shipped out. Horus, I was devastated.

"What brought it all to an end John?"

"Apparently in 1831 one hundred and sixty-eight years ago a violent storm came ashore into the area and flooded it out. It killed some slaves and a couple of the Petersons as well. The records were rewritten at that time except for the ones the land commission had that had mysteriously disappeared. The house was the only thing that survived. Peterson's land was destroyed but the slaves that survived rebuilt it. The family was grateful and began to treat their slaves like family. They bought a few more but never sold off another one, which is why so many people here in Buffalo Hill have never left or stayed away for good. Our spiritual connections are rooted very deeply.

Just then a siren went off. As I looked out my rearview mirror, nearly jumping out of my seat, I saw one of Augustus Hill's finest. This city within a city had it's own private bulldogs. The officer stepped out of the car with his hand on his holster and walked toward my car. I eyed him in the side view mirror and put both hands on the steering wheel. This cop could have been a spokesman for Butterball turkeys. He had a plain face with red cheeks mirror-framed shades and a hat that seemed tall as Hoss Cartwright's. He approached my side of the car and looked in. Before saying anything he looked up and down the street turned toward Peterson Mansion and then looked at me.

"Driver's license," he said.

I reached up slowly took my license and insurance registration off the visor and handed them to him.

"Be back," the officer said and went back to his patrol car.

I waited patiently as I looked down at the Peterson Mansion. I started to see images of men on horseback at the house. The street that led to the mansion suddenly became a dirt road. I shook my head and wiped my eyes to ward off any dizzy spell I may have been getting but the image continued. I saw men dressed as field workers with straw hats and pants that came just over the knees. Women carried baskets and some well-dressed people were standing on the front lawn under a tree. The images were barely visible but I saw a man with a big hat throw a rope over a branch.

I began to sweat I saw a woman being forced to stand on a short block kicking and swinging her arms trying to prevent her head from going in a noose. The lady screamed. I snapped out of it sweating and panting.

"Hey! Hey!" the officer yelled. "Are you on drugs?"

"No. Uh...just tired," I said.

"Go on get outta here!" The officer yelled.

I drove off. It was now 11:00 A.M. and I was about five minutes away from the ceremony. I reached over to my lunch bag and took out my sandwich and milk. I barely had an appetite, but I bit my sandwich and gulped down half of my milk. Still shaken by the vision I finished my sandwich and washed it down with the remainder of milk. I savored how refreshing the milk was, wiped my mouth with a napkin and left it there as if I were going to throw up. I slowed the car down and came to a stop not believing what I saw before me.

The crowd was overwhelming. Every local media outlet was there. There were T.V. stations, radio stations, and local newspapers. Some of the most notable television anchor personnel had live coverage of the ceremony opponents. The radio stations had set up canopies and tents next to their vans giving away T-shirts, buttons, caps, and movie passes for the theater that would not open for seven more months. Of the local black radio stations, all but one bought into this event.

I looked around and then got out of my car turning from side to side. I started making my way through the crowd thick with reporters and journalists. Some of them recognized me from other events when the Southside Community Center had protested. They would have loved to ask me what I thought of the event but their bosses would not have put my response on the air or in print unless it followed some type of verbal or physical altercation with an opposing group. I walked through the media's tents shaking my head. I made my way over to the oppositions camp-the community center where grass-root organizations and a few church groups were picketing by forming a circle and chanting.

"Don't hate! Relocate!" "Don't hate! Relocate!" "Don't hate! Relocate!"

Some of the protesters and members of the community center recognized me. I gave hugs and handshakes. Camara, a co-worker of mine, was like my twin. We saw eye to eye on many issues and projects in the community. She approached me with an update of the ceremony.

"Hotep! RA!"

"Hotep! Camara. What's happening?" I replied.

"The police officers have instructed us to remain behind the barriers as long as we protest. The only way we can get any closer is to drop the signs and keep quiet," she said.

Suddenly the attention shifted toward the rear where a stage had been built for the celebrity guests and sponsors. A caravan of limos pulled up. I used my height to my advantage and looked over the crowd.

I told Camara, "Go tell the others I'm going to work my way up front where the guests can see me."

She asked, "Why are you going away from the group? Do you want me to answer any questions reporters might ask? What about those elders who depend on your presence?"

I said, "I need you to hold down the front." Tell the reporters just how you feel and you won't say anything wrong. The elders will be fine as long as they remain close to the group. But trust me; something tells me I need to go up front.

She said, "If that's the way you feel Ra then who am I to question those instincts of yours. Good luck!"

I gave her a hug, then started making my way through the crowd. I glanced at my watch it was 11:15 A.M. I was still not exactly sure why I had to go up front. Maybe it was something Miss Imani had said, or something was related to my vision, but I knew I had to. It was as if something more powerful than myself guided me, directing my every step.

The crowd thickened as I drew closer to the front and people turned around to see where this force of movement came from. As they turned and saw me, I knew there would be no comment about my pushing. Most of them were Northside residents black and white who saw me as a troublemaker. As I made it to the front line, I noticed two black police officers were making sure no one went under or over the rope. There was a five-foot gap between the rope line and the celebrity stage. The two officers glanced at each other and gestured to indicate "Mr. Trouble" yours truly was here. They then turned to me and starred as if I was the worst kind of African. They had seen me in action before: at rallies, marches, and other types of protests. To them, I was not the hero the Southside had made me out to be. I was a throwback to the sixties. A dinosaur not willing to totally assimilate into the mainstream or buy into the development plans for the black historical area. To them I was just another brother lost in a world of black people who were too afraid and too lazy to change.

The moment had arrived for the guests to enter onto the stage. I saw them waving their hands, their fake smiles gleaming at the unconscious people in the crowd. Flash bulbs popped and T.V. cameras rolled. These were Buffalo Hill's cream-of-the-crop citizens, better-known-as "Sambos."

Chapter II

BEGINNING OF THE PAST

A lady approached the microphone that sat on the podium in the middle of the stage. Her name was Virginia Peterson, Bob Peterson's wife. She was the creme-de-la-creme of Buffalo Hill's social community. She raised money for a lot of good causes but none that benefited the Southside. I had met her on a few occasions and was always pleased with our conversations. She was the perfect corporate executive wife. She gave him three spoiled-ass children and showed no indication that she could think on her own. She began to introduce the guests. As they started up the stairs that led to their seats on the stage, I looked at them one by one.

The first one up was the Sambo who invited the others to come, the Reverend A. J. Bookman, the Black Messiah, God's gift to black people of this city. He had left the community years ago to live up on the hill. His kids attended a private school, yet he regarded public education as a trial and tribulation that was good for the soul. He was a devout promoter of organized religion. Having no connection to spirituality, his motto was "You can have what I have if you have the faith that I have," convincing his followers they could also be economically prosperous in a capitalistic society. Yeah right! He wore designer suits and lots of gold jewelry; he owned expensive cars and had both a helicopter and a jet. Rev had stopped fighting alongside black people for justice years ago, now he just advises them to pray, i.e. 'Jesus will take care of it.' He considered me, of all people, a setback for African people. I once was an avid churchgoer, but after asking serious questions about my spirituality, one of my answers was that religion and man-made doctrine would no longer push me toward my higher self. So I had told Rev that I graduated from church and religion and that he should be happy for me.

The next person who walked up the stairs was Kerry "Crossover" Collins. He had two years of college and has been in the NBA for four years. Although born and raised in the hood, he has not been back since. He is flashy, brash, cocky and a sincere egotist. His idea of a great fan was one who bought his shoes and tickets to see him play. He liked to see women in skirts and brothers in his shirt. All he thought about was basketball, partying, sex and money. Kerry had three illegitimate kids, with whom he had no contact, except for child support payments. His white agent setup his charities, none of which helped blacks or the community from which he came. He showed up for this event only because his agent had invested some of his money in the theater. He waved to the crowd with one hand, the other holding the hand of a very slender white woman. He glanced at me momentarily thinking he might know me because of my height but realized who I was from TV reports and shook his head. In Kerry's mind, I was a real "nigger." Mainly due to the fact I didn't treat him or any professional athlete like the second coming and that I was not bound by any "House Negro's" contract where I could not speak my mind. He walked onto the podium with a sway in his walk and took his seat. His girlfriend sat close to him.

The next person was Aaron Thomas, known throughout the hip-hop community as "Black Dawg," a true soldier - yeah right! He was a rap artist and one of the biggest exploiters of positive black images. His lyrics were violent toward so-called haters and sexually explicit toward women. Most of his lyrics were considered toned-down but were still suggestive, such as, 'I wined and dined ya. You should let me get behind ya'. Aaron grew up in a well-to-do household, graduated from high school and a junior college. He had a well-paying job, but quit to pursue a rap career. He did very well. It's just that he raps about how hard it was growing up in the streets, and hanging out with drug-dealers, yet no one in the hood remembers that version. Most of his homies were out of work and riding his jock (sucking up, sort of speak). He wore about ten thousand dollars in jewelry; four neck-laces, one about the size of a hubcap, three rings on one hand and two on the other; and two large bracelets, one on each wrist. He lived a lifestyle that kept him one paycheck from poverty. He wore a shirt with cut off sleeves to sport his tat-toos and his upper right arm bore a crucifix, as if he knew what that meant. He walked across the stage holding a peace sign, not saying a word and looking straight-faced behind those shades. The slogan on his shirt read, "Keeping it real," "Real dumb," I thought. The tragedy of this was that Aaron was a smart young man. He was just riding out a fad. He walked over and gave Kerry a high five, as if they shared a common bond. I knew the only thing they had in common was that they grew up three blocks apart and in my mind they were both a disgrace to the community.

Not far behind Dawg was his partner in crime, the one person that I had constantly tried to save, Katherine Davis, or as she had became to be known as, Couchie Kat." Kat was discovered by Dawg and is a member of the rap game in which he is associated. I knew her parents when she crashed into me while riding her bike as a kid. She had scraped her knee pretty bad and I took her home. I watched her blossom into a young adult and struggle with herself in the process. She was still wholesome inside but had sold out to support her two kids. Her children were by two different men who would not support them. They both had returned to be with her and her newfound fame, but she "dissed" them because she had labeled herself as, "The New Black Queen, the in-tell-i-gent woman on the scene." She wanted to be the C.E.O. of her own record label but was closer to being a HO. Kat gave peace signs from both hands as she walked across the stage, her long legs coated with baby oil. Switching like a model on a Paris runway, her motions captivated Rev Bookman, Kerry and Aaron. They stared at her like hungry wolves stare at sheep. Kat walked over to Kerry and surprisingly kissed him. She did this in hopes that it would stir up some sort of controversy that would start rumors. What she didn't know was as beautiful and caramel as her skin tone was, it would never be light enough for Kerry to be seen with her. The only thing she was to him was a quick piece behind closed doors, like the three different mothers of his children. Kat waved to Rev Bookman who never made eye contact with her, but stared at her legs and midsection baring a red rose at the top of her cleavage. His old hormones were racing as he put his eyes on her see-through mesh blouse that was open. Kerry and rap duo Aaron along with Kat were here to help convince the youngsters that this new theater was going to be "deaf," and was only going to show the "krunkest" movies around.

The next to be introduced was not really a major celebrity, but well known in other circles, Elizabeth Calloway. We both attended high school together but didn't know each other that well. I had heard through the community grapevine that she believed in some of the things that I stood for but she was just too conscious of her image, so she kept quiet. Elizabeth graduated valedictorian in high school, attended Texas Southern University receiving a law degree. She owned a law firm and was voted businesswoman of the year by the Buffalo Hills Chamber of Commerce. She was smart as she was sharp, a very classy dresser with a beautiful chocolate complexion as rich as you could imagine. She was dedicated to her career. This was one of the reasons she had not met "Mr. Right." The other is that she is looking for someone who may not conform. She gave an interview once in a local magazine saying her ideal man was single with no kids, well-educated, made good money, sensitive yet masculine, and totally into his woman. Elizabeth did not sincerely want to be here but came because she won the Chamber of Commerce Award. She couldn't stand corporate functions, thought Kat was a disgrace, and despised the thought of sitting next to her even though the feeling was mutual. The Rev to her was nothing but a money hungry, fake religious man who was going to burn in hell. She felt Kerry was just an overpriced ignorant jock, and she hated seeing that white woman on his arms. She sat down, did not speak to anyone and quickly smiled at them. As she sat, we made eye contact; she smiled, as did I. I thought to myself, "Well, well, look at Miss Thang."

The last guest to come up was the public relations manager for Peterson Industries, my former co-worker and assistant, Ward B. Shaw, the biggest Sambo in Buffalo Hill. Ward was in my group that worked on the portfolio five years ago for Founder's Day. I had found out later, through a friend, that Ward called Bob Peterson the minute we returned from D.C. and told him everything. Ward had since been promoted into my old position. We were once associates but not very close friends. Even then, I never really trusted him. He tried too hard to convince Peterson that he was a team player. I knew that he was the most dangerous kind of man to be around. He had a wife whom he married, because he got her pregnant. He has since come to resent her because she appears too black. Her broad nose and thick lips tended to embarrass him, so he talked her into getting a nose job. He pays to send her to the beauty shop weekly to keep her naturally kinky hair straight, but there was a time when he thought it was okay to sleep or to be seen with her, because no other woman wanted him. Now, he thinks his stuff don't stink. He was a conservative Republican who visited his people in the neighborhood only during the holidays.

We glimpsed at one another for only a brief moment and those few seconds said everything. I knew this brother was a sorry ass excuse for a man. Ward quickly walked across the stage and got a look from the others that was real cool. The way he was skinning and grinning, I don't blame them.

Last up was Bob Peterson, my former boss. He had given me my first start in corporate America and I thank him for that but I wasn't prepared for the aggression and deceit it took to survive in it. Also I had learned something about Bob. He never really amounted up to the expectations of his father and great forefathers. His decision-making had not always been that great and, at times, the board of trustees rejected the ideas he presented to them. I feel as though Bob would have let us tell the true story of his family but the pressure of his family and the board was just too great. He needed to do something big to prove to his father, Bob Peterson, Sr., that he was worthy to run the company, so he came up with the idea about the theater. He also knew the only way to pull it off was to raise those "Black Dollars." He knew he had to get black people who were admired by the community, never commenting on the fact that the theater was going to be built on an old burial ground. His only comment, "The good Rev

Bookman had seen to it that he would be forgiven for any wrong-doing." Rev Bookman was the spokesperson for the whole project and had gotten all the celebrities and guests together; Peterson was smart enough to get the right Sambo to do the job.

He gave about a ten-minute speech on how the new theater would be a model. "Diversity in the workplace" "An employee who does an honest day's work will receive honest day's pay, and the rules are the rules, no special treatment," he said.

That speech was about as legitimate as a three legged chicken. The Peterson family had a hard time crossing over to diversity in the workplace; it showed in their good old boys board meetings. He ended his speech with the usual round of cheers and applause, and yelled, "Let the ground breaking begin!"

A mixture of cheers and boos began to ring out as Bob started down the steps; the guest and stars followed behind him. As each one approached the dig site, they were given gold painted shovels with green ribbons. It had been roped off for some time and dampened so the earth could be easily dug.

I checked my watch. It showed 11:50 A.M. Whatever Miss Imani said was going to happen at noon, was only ten minutes away. You know, Horus, seeing what the ceremony was all about, the mixture of townspeople who supported it, and the power and influence of the Peterson's for nearly two hundred years made me pause in wonderment. "I couldn't help but doubt if all this protesting was done in vain. I mean they had the numbers you know, and Miss Imani told me about what was supposed to happen to save this situation. I loved her dearly Horus, but I thought that she had really lost it. You know?"

"Yeah John, I know. Look my friend's business sent me out of town last weekend. I didn't come back here to get a week's old story about how you punked out. Now you said you thought Miss Imani was out of it. What happened next?"

"You're right Horus." No sooner had I checked my watch when the guest of the hour started over to the ceremonial mound to dig. A loud rumble came from the sky. Now I know you had heard about the freak storm during this event but it was much more than that.

Everyone was looking around; some looked up wondering what had happened. Others thought it was thunder but there was no rain in the forecast for days.

"There's not a cloud in the sky," said a reporter.

I looked at the guests who were aligning themselves with the cameras for their ceremonial dig or, as I know it to be, "the desecration of the burial ground." There was another rumble of thunder that was louder and seemed to last a few seconds longer.

A gentleman from the main newspaper shouted, "My God! Would you look at that!" He was looking up and pointing to the sky at a big black cloud. I couldn't believe it. I thought about what Miss Imani had told me. Suddenly a gust of wind came strong enough to blow hats off the crowd.

Rev Bookman yelled out, "Lord, Lord what is going on?"

Virginia Peterson quickly grabbed the microphone insisting, "Everyone please remain calm!"

People couldn't help but notice. The cloud was closer and even darker. The wind began to pick up. I checked my watch again it was 11:55. It was quite evident that whatever Miss Imani had told me, was happening. I glanced at the cloud. It was directly overhead blocking out the sun. In the cloud I began to see an image form. It was a woman and she wore an African headdress made for a queen. The wind began to blow fiercely but I couldn't take my eyes off the cloud. I began to hear African drums and chants in the distance. I turned to see, who was playing them but there was no one. My heart was racing and people were running for cover in fear of a freak storm. The drums continued growing louder. They seemed to be coming from the ceremonial mound. I heard Bob yell out in desperation, "Dig I say! And get those cameras going!" Why in the world would he insist on digging at a time like this was strange indeed.

My watch read 11:59. Without any further thought I leaped over the boundary rope and ran for the panel yelling out to them to stop. They still had shovels in their hands neither digging or hearing what I was saying.

A policeman and an event official came after me, but I ran. Using long strides with my arms stretching out back and forth I ran as fast as I could. I stumbled onto the mound where the panel stood, knocking over cameras and reporters. As I stood up, Bob and the panel placed their shovels into the ground. It was as if everything was in slow motion. I reached for Bob's shovel. The drums were still playing loudly. Suddenly a loud rumble came from the cloud that was frightening and in a split second a lightening bolt hit the mound.

The drums had stopped and the voices of the people in chaos had disappeared. It became silent and still. I felt like I was not touching the ground. It was very cold and dark. I couldn't see my hand in front of me. I could only hear myself breathe. I then realized I was suspended somehow but I wasn't floating or anything. There was no ground beneath me. I tried to talk but no voice came out.

The silence of darkness was still present. My mind began to wonder about what could have happened. The vision that Miss Imani had told me about made me remember the "KA." Maybe this was what I was going through - that vital energy which creates and sustains life - a transformation of my body.

I began to hear voices that seemed far away. The ground was back under my feet. I no longer felt like I was on a roller coaster. The voices seemed to be getting closer. I tried to speak again. Finally, I could hear myself. A light appeared to be forming like a sunrise, but much faster. A sharp pain ran through me.

It was daylight wherever I was. I looked around and there they were Kerry, Aaron, Kat, Elizabeth, and Ward. Their mouths were opened wide. The look on their faces was of shock and disbelief. No one could explain our whereabouts or what had happened. Confusion was mounting. We were not alone; there were other people standing near us, their heads bowed in prayer. At the forefront was Rev Bookman, looking very strange. The people raised their heads as we started to regain our faculties.

"Whad da hell is dis?" Aaron shouted. They started to talk.

"Hey, what is dis? Whas gon on Lawd?" Rev said, "And why you and evabody dressed like dat?" referring to Elizabeth.

Elizabeth answered, "Use dressed kinda strange too."

We had apparently crossed over to somewhere but failed to bring our look of 1999 with us. Rev's thousand-dollar worth of gold rings, watches, crucifix, and expensive suit did not make it. He now had on a white shirt, ruffled with lace, black wool pants, black coat and boots. Dirty, white, ruffled shirts and wool knickers had replaced all Aaron's tattoos and hip-hop apparel. Kerry's high fashioned Italian suit and my casual urban look were gone. The fine shoes, Air Jordans and hiking boots were gone as well. We were now what black folks called "Buck Barefooted." Ward was dressed a little better. His corporate casual look of Dockers and a Polo shirt was now pants that came up around the ankles and a long sleeved shirt with a vest. He had on some dirty shoes that resembled the kind babies are trained to walk in.

The ladies were not any better. Their hairstyles and make-up were gone. Kat's mesh blouse and "Daisy Dukes" shorts were replaced with a long gray dress with red and blue flowers. The dress covered her from her neck to her feet. It fitted tightly around the neck, breast and waist, but flared out down to her feet. Her blonde wig had given way to a small Afro.

Elizabeth's skirt, blouse, and pumps were now replaced with nearly the same style of dress as Kat's, except, she had no collar and no flowers. She was barefoot, and her perm was permanently nappy. We looked at each other and ourselves in shock and disbelief.

Rev looked down and said, "Oh lawd, we done died and gone to heaven."

The people standing with us gestured for us to please be quiet.

"Shh! Ya'll gon get evabody in hot wadda," said a middle-aged woman standing next to Rev.

I looked around and said, "Naw Rev this ain't heaven. We in hell. I thank wees been thrown ova to da udder side."

"Udder side of whad?" said Kerry.

"John, what in da hell have you godden us into?" Kat said.

"Yeah fool, whad up wit all dis?" Aaron added.

I began to try and explain to them the only thing that I could think of was that the ancestors of Buffalo Hill, according to Miss Imani's vision, sent a black cloud over us during the ceremony, which was somehow responsible for our positions right now, but it didn't work.

They all stared at me like I was on serious drugs. Elizabeth was the first to reply. "You mean dat creepy old woman, who lives cross the street from you?"

"Man you must be out yo damn mind!" cried Aaron. Ward added very eloquently but with attitude, "Wees not here fo no udda reason sept fo some joke by you and dose sick-ass black folks you call comrades."

"Oh yeah!" I said, quickly eyeing all of them while walking towards Ward's face. "Den explain to me why wees all dress dis way and is talkin dis way and dose folks ova dere is lookin at us like we da crazy ones?"

Rev stopped me from going off on Ward. He pulled me by the arm and turned me around to see the other people frantically motioning for us to keep quiet. We caught the attention of a white man on a horse, which started riding towards us.

The middle-aged lady in the group spoke up again. "Will ya'll please hush up and stop acking crazy, oh day gon make us go to da fields or sumpin. Jus hush up."

"Hey ya'll chill out fo a second;" I said. "Let da lady do the talkin."

The man on horseback made his way over to us. He was steely eyed with a scratchy beard. He was dressed like an old western photo. He had a round white derby lodged on his head as if it were going to fall off. He stared at everyone while unbuckling a long-barreled rifle tied to his saddle. While holding the reins of the horse in one hand, he reached on to the saddle and retrieved the whip that was wrapped around the handgrip. With the whip in the other hand he looked at the woman who had tried to calm us down.

"Ressie!" he said in a strong voice. "I hear some yelling ova here. What the hell is going on?"

Ressie appeared nervous from the tone of the man's voice and the commotion from the gang and me.

She said to him, "Oh nudin really Massa Peterson!" My stomach began to turn from fear after what I heard. I spoke silently oh god! I had a very good idea where we might be.

She added, "Some of us is jus takin da death of Momma Raylene kinda hard das all Sur. Wees glad dat you and Massa Ugustus (referring to Augustus Peterson) gave us half da day, so wees can have a surmony fo Momma Raylene."

Master Peterson listened to Ressie but did not say okay. He looked over at the people and said, "If I have to come up here again, ya'll all won't like it, ya'll won't like it one bit." He turned his horse by the reins. "This funeral is ova!" The horse trotted away down the dirt road leading from the cemetery.

I walked over and stood next to Ressie. We watched as the man and the horse moved out of hearing distance. Everyone started talking, and the people who attended the burial wanted to know why we were acting so strangely, so crazy. The panel resumed their jabbering asking question after question. No one was listening to anyone. It was pure chaos.

I then shouted out to the gang, "Chill out!"

They began to calm down although they had frowns of confusion on their faces just as the other people who were wondering what 'chill out' meant. I took control with the lady Ressie by my side.

Apparently, we crossed a timeline and ended up in slavery times. "Miss Ressie what year is it?" I asked.

She looked at me like I was out of my mind. "Now, John you know dis is 1831. Whad is rong with chall? Momma Raylene is gone up to da heavens, but ain't no sence in ya'll gon crazy now."

She placed her hands on her hip, looking like the mother of everyone. She was a tall thin woman, dark-skinned with uneven small Afro bearing traces of gray. Her facial features were pure African-like someone out of "National

Geographic." The inside of her eyes were soft yellow with "crows feet" on each side, her teeth were bone white. There was not a trace of European blood in her. She was apparently a leader of some sort being singled out to speak for the people. They had begun to form behind her. I was curious about one thing so I asked. "How'd ju know my name?"

She looked even more puzzled, and angrily said, "Now, Boy, you looka here," shaking her finger at me. "You and da rest of dese here fools needs to ask da Lawd for some help real fast, aw ya'll gon be laying ova dere next to Momma Raylene."

I was catching on and starting to put the pieces together. I realized Ressie wasn't crazy. I had to believe her. For some strange reason, she reminded me of Miss Imani. I motioned for the gang to be cool. Checking out their shocked faces, I began to explain.

"Whether or not ya'll believe whad happened; it has, and dere is a reason why. I don't know exactly whad, but we needs to just calm down and thank fo a minute."

I did not tell them I had a pretty good idea what had happened. It didn't work earlier and I didn't think trying to explain any more of Miss Imani's vision would bring any more clarity to the situation. I realized their prejudice towards me would not allow them to believe anything I had to offer. So I had to use another approach. I turned to Ressie and said, "It's jus like you say, Momma, Raylene dyin' an all got us acking crazy."

She hesitated then said, "Well das okay baby, jus as long as you an da rest of dese fools is gon be alright. Uderwise we in fo a heap of trouble from Massa Peterson and dat henchman of his, Caleb."

"But before we go, Miss Ressie, just to make sure dat evabody is fine, let dem de...uh peoples know who de is," I said, pointing to the gang.

Ressie looked at me with a sharp eye, then grinning slyly on one side of her mouth showing a few of those bone white teeth. At that moment it seemed as though she knew exactly who we were and why I had asked. Hesitating a little she said, "Okay John, if you say so." She turned to the gang. "Whadeva it is dat is gon make ya'll ack right." She started with Rev Bookman, "Now, dat dere is Walla, but we calls him Rev. He was one of the fus slaves ta git here. Massa Ugusta names him Walla cuz he so plump, looked like he had walled wit da hogs."

The people on hands chuckled a little obviously not believing the seriousness of what had happened. Rev didn't find it funny at all.

"Yep," said Ressie. "Walla done been here twendy-eight years now, wuks up in da big house, takes care of old man Ugusta and preacha's da wud four him"

"Damn!" says Aaron. "Rev you ain't nudding but a house nigger." Ressie, not knowing, "House nigger" was a pejorative term, replied in Rev's defense, "Yea, but hees a goodun doe."

The rest of us held back any comments we might have had, as. Rev was being belittled.

Ressie continued, "Now dat dere K-ree," pointing to Kerry. "Massa bought him here when he was ten years ole to wuk da field and grows up ta make young uns - lots of um since he so tall and strong."

Kerry loudly said, "Waid, Waid! Whole up! Dis ain't even cool."

I immediately ran over to Kerry, grabbed him around the shirt, looked at him, and said, "Man I suggest you go along wit dis til wees find out whas gon on here." I then turned to the rest of them talking low to where only they could hear me. "Wees all are gonna haf to go along wit dis. If wees don't, then wees could scare dese people enough to get us killed. Now, do ya'll want dat? Huh? Let's jus take whadeva gets thrown at us till wees find our way out." They mumbled with a little discomfort.

"Yeah das cool." Said a disgruntled Kerry, forcing himself to agree.

I waited for the rest of them to comply.

"Cool, man," said Aaron.

"Yeah I guess," answered Ward. The rest of them nodded their heads in agreement. I walked back over to Ressie who still seemed puzzled by all of us.

"Please continue Miss Ressie."

"Likes I wuz saying, K-ree has tree chilun. Two boys dat wuks in da fields wit him, and a gul who wuks in da big house."

"Whad!" Kerry screamed.

"Man, be cool!" I replied.

Ressie continued, "Dat dere is Aron. Massa buys him when he was a young un too to wuk in da fields. Massa don't trust him much doe, use eder John, eva since yo Momma Pauline tried to run away with you and Aaron years ago. Massa thanks das still inside ya'll head. Das why Massa Peterson wuz down dere listnun to whad it is wees doin up here. Figa use and Aaron gone get some crazy idea bout running off?" Ressie then pointed at Kat and Elizabeth. "Nah dose two wuz bone here on da plantation, but de carries on like two ol hens sometimes. Kathy wuks up in da big house and Lizzy wuks in da fields."

Elizabeth replied, "Hm."

The expression on Ressie's face quickly changed, as did some of the other slaves as she began to mention whom Ward was. She gave him an evil stare.

"Well, well, I thought you wouldn't even had da guts to come up here you ole backbiter."

Ward looked shock. "Whad I do?" he asked.

"How can you even sho yo face in dis cemetery wheah you done put enough of us, you ol Judas!" said a woman from the crowd. We all looked puzzled.

I asked Ressie curiously, "Wad ol Ward do?"

She turned, looked at me angrily, and said, "How can you even speak to him afta whad he don did to you?"

I stopped Ressie from continuing; I said, "Okay, okay, Miss Ressie, let's jus gone on."

She turned to the hands, about thirty of them young and old, light-skinned and dark-skinned. A couple was dressed like house servants including Rev and Kat. The others were dressed like they worked strictly hard labor, resembling Aaron, Kerry, Elizabeth, and me. Ward was dressed up like the white man, Master Peterson, who was on horseback. She began to walk off and they followed behind her.

I said to her, "We be right behind you Miss Ressie but I got to talk to dese folks here bout sumpin."

She waved me off, never turning back. Just then Ward stepped up. "Man wees has got to get da hell outa here soon."

"Yeah," Aaron said. "If I think we are where I think we are den I know I'm fen to go down dere and get my ass wuped to det cuz ain't no white man gone call me "niggah" and tells me whad to do!"

"Oh really!" I said. "Dose white record bosses tells you whad to do all the time and you get called "niggah" all da day long. But if a ass wupin is whad you want, den a ass wupin is what you gone get down dere."

Aaron got quiet; he stared at me, then bowed and shook his head rumbling on about how this situation is not cool at all.

I told the gang, "Look, from here on out we got to go by our real names, and we show cain't do nothing bout da way we is talkin. Now, when we go down to da plantation wees all got new lives wheder we likes it or not. Don't go down dere shucking and jiving, like some know it all, and get wuped wit dat whip Massa Peterson had or shot wit dat shotgun of his. Don't you ladies go sassing and get raped or sumpin. Is dis all clear to evabody?"

Rev said, "Hey, John, are you sho you know whad is going on?"

"Yeah Rev, I'se thank I do know, but you can better believe we'ze ain't gon find no ansah standing here."

Kerry blurted out, "Come on John, man! Dis can't be hapnin to us. I mean dis ain't da dam "X-Files". Dis is slavery times man. Ain't nobody here is prepared to handle white folks like dose kind on dat plantation. I mean white folks ain't neva done nudin to me; nair one of um neva called me no niggah. Dis is crazy, man."

"Use might be called a niggah all da time. You just ain't listnin to um," said Elizabeth with an attitude.

Kerry gave her the finger. I knew where she was coming from with her comment; and I thought, Man, would I love to take it from here. But I knew this was not the time or place for it.

Elizabeth thought otherwise though. She came back at Kerry. "Member dat lockout ya'll pro ballplayers had? Dat wuz da clearest message whad de tought of ya'll."

"Dat's not da case," Kerry said. "Wees got sumpin outta dat deal."

Elizabeth replied, "Dat wuz da bes time fo ya'll to stawt you own damn league."

I then jumped in. "Okay you two dat is enough. Da last thang we need is to be divided. So, can you two jus shut up till weze figa out hows we gon handle all of dis?"

Kerry wanted to answer but hesitated as if he were at a lost for words. He didn't know how to handle a strong-spirited woman like Elizabeth so he angrily responded to me. "Don't tell me to shutup. Besides, niggahs cain't get tegeder fo nothing anyhows. Das why I'm gone stays right dey wid dose wite folks, dat stands next to me."

I really wanted to give this Sambo a piece of my mind, but I knew it would be irrelevant. I motioned with my hands for him to calm down. I said, "Look man, if dat's how you feel den fine. But, da only thang dat use gon set to "crossup" here is dat concept you got. Da Africans aw da only ones you got now. If you thank dose 1831 white folks down dere is gon back you up, you gon be hangin and swangin brudder. Take a look at hows you dressed. Use a field nigger now. Dat means de distrust you mo dan anybody. So, likes I say, we needs to get it togeder fo we get in serious trouble. Is!….. dat!.... clear?" They all appeared to agree, nodding their heads as I surveyed their faces. Kerry's anger had turned into embarrassment, although he stayed silent. "Now, we need to head on down to da plantation, befo we be missed."

"Hey, John, man, I'm kinda scayed. I'se don't know if I can handle all of dis man; I just don't know," Ward said, looking teary-eyed. "Miss Ressie done already said I'se kinda a bad person and I'se don't know wuz in stow fo me down dere."

Elizabeth walked up to me, "Say brudder, I fo one believe dat you knows whad's up fo us."

Kat said, "Yeah John. As long as I'se known you, you always done known more dan whad you let's folk believe."

"Well," I said, I'se do know a little, and I feel our ancestas is trying to tell us sumpin. I'se don't know fo sho, but I do feel. De only way wese gon get ansahs is on dat plantation down dat road. And Ward use mite as well stop crying cuz whadeva you done did it wuzn't against no white folks cause you still alive. Member ya'lls name now. Damn! I hate talkin dis here way. Let's go ya'll."

They were scared as they started down the road, as was I; but what scared me the most were the people who in my mind were nothing more than community sellouts, Sambos. They were not cognizant of what the atrocities of this time could bring, and how it could affect someone's state of mind. You would think I would be the one to snap and lose it, but it was my faith in what Miss Imani told me and my knowledge of our ancestors and history that was keeping me sane. So here I was in 1831, the only person who fully knew the conditions of our people in this day and time, leading a group of Africans whom I had despised, who despised me and each other. I didn't feel hopeful that we would make it out, not together anyway. I thought that maybe I should just use my knowledge to save myself. It was frightening.

The gang walked close by me, including my Sambo former co-worker, Ward. I knew Ward was not to be trusted, past or present. Again, the brother was in the most vulnerable position to sell out. I knew he must have done something to the slaves for Miss Ressie to talk to him that way. The answer lay somewhere in the slave quarters of the plantation. I glanced over at Rev. I knew that every sermon he preached, every soul he had saved, every white person he had done good for, could not prepare him for the ungodly hate he was about to encounter. There was not a language he could use that could change the thoughts and ways of this "peculiar institution." I looked back at Aaron and saw the confusion in his walk, the doubt in his eyes; the normal hip-hop flare and language he spoke might cost him his life. The clothes he was accustomed to wearing were gone; shirts that contained explicit rap logos and designer jeans that sagged below his hips, were of another time. He reminded me of the tamed little kid I knew in the hood, Aaron Anthony Thomas, Clyde and Janelle Thomas' baby boy. I knew I had to stay on him, so the wanna be gangster character he portrayed, wouldn't cost him his life. Kerry walked on the side of Aaron looking scared as well, lacking the pride of the NBA. He has four years in the league to stand on. He was a three-time all-star thinking he had it all, the game, the money, cars, homes and women. But the person he admired the most, other than himself, was Aaron, mainly because he was a better rapper. I knew Kerry would find it hard to handle a wife and three kids. He would probably have to make the biggest adjustment of all to plantation life. His agent, or brain, wouldn't be here to think for him. He was going to have to make decisions not just for himself, but also for his family as a husband and father.

The road started to wind and I sensed that we were near. Even though it was 168 years earlier the smell of people and life in Buffalo Hill was the same. I glanced to my right. Kat was so close to me I could barely swing my long arms. Elizabeth was close to my left; I was going to have to be both big brother and father to these two beautiful, talented and misguided sisters. Every negative opinion they had of black men would be exploited, live and in living color. They would see first-hand how to break a man and make a nigger - the root of why most black men are the way they are. Kat grabbed my arm around my elbow. She looked up at me with her soft brown eyes, since her blue contacts didn't make the trip. She smiled with her voice trembling with fear. "You know, you promised my folks dat you would look out for me."

"I'd lay down my life fo you Kat. You know use my lil sista," I said. She playfully rested her head on my upper arm feeling a bit of strength already. I had hoped Kat's flirtatious and hoochie Momma ways missed the trip. They wouldn't work or be understood in this day and time. That personality she had developed at twenty-six was only the result of a society that had replaced morals and values with attitudes and debauchery. She was the product of young men's fantasies. Elizabeth inched closer. I extended my arm out like the father of the bride. I told her, "Whad I said to Kat goes fo you too Lizzy." She smiled only a little. I knew she was frightened but she wasn't the kind to show it.

"Ya still got ways wit da ladies, John boy."

Elizabeth's intelligence, attitude, and strength would be challenged here. All the inspiration she had to help her achieve in a male dominated society could come crumbling down. The strength that it took to get where she was in law would have to become more spiritual now.

The road started to change, and in the distance the echoes of farm life began. My heartbeat increased while Kat and Lizzy squeezed my arm tighter. I could barely walk. Their fear was mounting as well. "Hey! Listen up." I said. "I needs ya'll to be strong now and believe evathang is gone be alright." The road was no longer rough, but flat and smooth. Trees grew evenly on both sides. I glanced at them, looked back, looked again. "Dees are pecan trees!"

"Yeah, so whad?" said Rev.

I didn't answer Rev because I was trying to remember where I had seen all this before.

Kat said, "Whad is it John? You know sumpin?"

Aaron said, "Hey, man. If it's wuth anythang, I'se believe in ya knowledge of us black folk. But man please don't leave us out if ya know sumpin."

Aaron's voice was trembling. He was a scared young man. Not the one who usually held his peace while sipping on a forty ounce of malt liquor, not fearing anything. I answered them easing the tension.

"I can't tell ya'll evathang cause I have not put all da pieces togeder yet. Fo da most pawt I know it won't be good to tell ya'll evathang cause den dose white folks can hold it against evabody else, includin the black folk we still hafta meet. But whad I can tell ya'll is dat dese rows of pecan trees sho looks familiar. If my mind is still in awdor we are walking down Peterson's way, headed fo da big mansion."

Rev checked it out. "Ya know John, I believe use right. I done drove dis way a few times for de functions dat da Petersons has gave."

Just then Kerry nervously said, "Man, dis getting scary by da steps wees taking."

"It ain't gon get no bedder if we don't stay strong," I replied.

Ward asked, "Why does ya thank it's not good to tell us whad is happnin, John?"

I said, "you see Ward, wheder it's 1831 or 1999, some white folks still make some of us African folk thank dat wees bedder off dan udder African folk and some African folks believe dat. Dey tells us to be a "team playa," so we believe dis and sometime wees get our brudders and sistas in lot's of trouble and dey makes use thank dat use done a good thang. So, until I'se get some ansuhs, it may be best dat da less ya'll know, da better it be." I said this to protect them, but they were grown, so I understood their need to know their fate.

Kerry asked me, "Well, Mr. African, how will we know who to talk to?"

I heard Kerry and shook my head.

Just then Kat looking straight at Rev yet speaking to Kerry, "Das easy. Da ones dat is close to Massa and all ways up in white folks face skinning and grinnin."

Lizzy added, "And da one dat talks a whole lot and acks a whole lot of questions," glancing at Kat.

I smiled, "Well, I thank dat da women gon be fine."

Rev answered bitterly, "Now, dat is wrong of ya'll to thank dat anybody gon sellout or sumpin. Sometimes folks gooda do whad dey godda do."

"Yeah, maybe in a very small way," I said. "But here dis may mean da difference to us gon home or stayin here for da rest of our lives. Member, some of dese black folk ain't gon trust you cuz dey been made not too. So it's impawdont when I say we got to know who da Sambo's are."

We slowed down and then came to a complete stop. Our mouths wide open as we stood nervous and in fear, butterflies in our bellies ready to be thrown up. As we stood there shaking not saying a word to each other the silence spoke volumes. We were in awe. There it was the Peterson mansion or in this time the largest and most populated antebellum plantation in Texas.

Chapter III

LIFE ON A PLANTATION

There it sat at the end of the road like a majestic palace. It wasn't the well-manicured lawn of the future, but its snow-white paint glowed brightly bringing to mind the essence of southern plantation life. We were witnessing the original mansion. It had no flaws. Its structuring was precise. I realized my information, as to who built this, was correct. Only the hands of pure African slaves, the first masons of the world, could have made those bricks fit into the frame like that of the pyramids. Its white columns resembled something out of an Egyptian dynasty. They appeared strong like the trunk of an oak tree. According to its history, it took them over five years to build this house. There was a swing on the porch just as I remembered when I visited here. Bluebonnets, roses, and all sorts of colorful flowers draped the steps that lead up to the porch. The grounds were not masterfully shaven like today's mansion, but they were still fertile with deep green shrubbery and magnolia trees scattered about.

We headed up the road that began to fork to the right which was no longer well paved it was rigged with potholes, bumps and well traveled cartwheel tracks. The neatly paved road continued to the mansion. The road we were on became rough. It started to wind away about two hundred or more yards from the house. A large oak tree stood to the side of the road and standing under it was Miss Ressie.

"Founds ya'll way back, huh?" she said.

"Yes mam," I answered, "Glad you waided on us."

"Um-huh," said Ressie. "I'se jus standin here talkin to dis ol oak tree waitun for ya'll to come up da road. Dis ol tree got lots of stories too. It tells me whad I need to know. Um-huh, yes suh. Well, let's gone on to da qwadas."

We headed for the slave quarters. I asked Ressie, "Whad did dat ol oak tree say?" She smiled at me and grabbed my hand; I suddenly felt cold chills that made my eyes nearly roll up in my head. I felt full, like someone had just poured water in my stomach; then it went away. I looked at Ressie who starred at me briefly with a coy look on her face as if she knew I was hiding something.

"Um-huh," she said, turning back toward the road. "Dat ol tree says use got lots of questions."

As we continued down the winding road, I began to fall under the spell of this haunting place. The gang appeared to be as I was, checking out the barn on the left. The smell of burned iron was apparently the work of a blacksmith. The fowl odors from animals were also circulating. On the right, several hundred rows of corn, so evenly grown, seemed to go on forever and ever each stalk kissing each other at the flow of the wind.

We continued on to the quarters. The little shack houses began to appear in the distance. While getting closer we could hear the voices of people speaking in broken English. The language of that day, that some of us now call "Ebonics." Just then we came to a stop. About fifty yards in front of us were the slave quarters - known only to the slaves as the back houses or quite simply, home. There were about fifteen of them made into the shape of a crooked box. Some of the little houses sat on bricks that were chipped. The others sat on oak stumps that appeared to have been placed there. We began to walk again. The quarters were setup like the letter

T. There were seven houses on each side with a larger one on the right end. A few hands, as they were called, peered out from around the long wool blankets that served as doors. I could feel tension and fright among the gang. Kat began to whimper, crying softly and covering her mouth as tears streamed down her face. She squeezed my arm tighter. Some of the hands stepped down out of the houses surveying us carefully. They didn't seem too surprised to see us. I could hear the gulps coming from Kerry and Ward. Aaron and Lizzy were quiet. They were trying to show strength.

Rev began to pray, "Oh merciful God in heaven, please hep us as we walk in the valley of Satan's work."

"Why is dey looking at us like dat?" asked Lizzy.

I again tried to ease some of the tensions. "Eva thang's gon be fine. Dey jus came out to see if wees okay. I'se assume word done spread dat we wuz ackin crazy ova at da cemetery." "Crazy is right," Ressie said. "Dey just wanna see if ya'll looks any diffrunt, das all."

We reached the end of the clearing. On the left we sat down at the first of five long tables with benches. It was a worn down clearing that had a well, a big cast iron pot, and two long poles. After canvassing the area we noticed two boys and a girl running towards us as fast as they could laughing all the way. We could hear them yelling, "Papa" "Papa," as they got closer to our group.

They stopped abruptly in front of Kerry. We were all stunned. Kerry's mouth had dropped completely and he immediately stood up.

The little girl said, "Papa, are use okay?" Her voice, meek and light was spoken with pure sincerity of concern for her father. Kerry, who was at a total loss for words, didn't have a clue what to say or do next. The two boys were each holding a leg - Kerry turned to me as if he needed some advice, but I shrugged my shoulders.

Kat came to his rescue. "Don't jus stand dere. Pick yo child up and let huh no huh pappy okay!"

Kerry glanced at the girl, who was his daughter, then at us, then back at the girl. Her dark brown eyes sparkled as she held her hand over her forehead like she was saluting to keep the sun out of her face. Kerry picked up the little girl as Kat had instructed not knowing her name or what to say.

The girl gave him a big kiss on the cheek. "Don't worry Papa. I hep Moma cook use a pa-te-ta pie," she said, while smiling and feeling secure in the arms of her father.

Kerry was uncomfortable and embarrassed. He probably had never held any of his three kids and it showed. As he put the girl back down on the ground, she began to look at him strangely.

"Papa," she said, "You didn't even kiss me."

Kerry was puzzled. "Well, I... I... Papa got a lot of thangs on his mind right now, okay. So why don't you and yo brudders go run along … gone now."

The girl just starred at Kerry. She bowed her head down and appeared to start crying. As she began rubbing her eyes, Kat got up, went over and squatted down to comfort her.

"Don't cry baby," she said. Yo pappy jus a lil sad cuz Moma Raylene done gone to heaven and he ain't gon sees huh no mo, das all."

She hugged the little girl and looked up at Kerry rolling her eyes in disgust.

"Man, you odda be shame of yo self. At least give the child a kiss," said Lizzy.

Kerry again turned toward me. "Gone on man," I said, "use should be use to it any hows."

"Yeah. Gone on man," added Rev.

Kerry bent down as Kat slowly released the girl. As she turned to her father, head still bowed, he picked her up and gave her a big kiss on the forehead. She flashed a huge grin and playfully pointed to her fat little cheek. Kerry obliged with another kiss. The scene was a little moving. I could tell from the expressions on everyone's face and the quaint sound of laughter that a little tension had left our hearts. It was well needed. While this was taking place Ressie was checking us out. She hadn't smiled through any of this but I could tell she had kept a close eye. Standing there with her left foot forward and right hip pointed outward; her left arm resting under her breast and right hand pinching and rubbing her chin. She had the look of contemplation and curiosity.

Then in the midst of our laughter she said, "Huh, name is Iris!"

Kerry hesitated as he put Iris down.

Ressie told the kids, "Ya'll chilin's gone on in da house."

The two boys finally released Kerry's legs. One of them said, "Miss Ressie, can we go play by da well?"

Ressie waited to answer, then said, "Ya'll asks yo' pappy."

The kids turned to Kerry who had a look like he had been asked the hardest question of his life.

"Uh.... uh.... I-I-I guess so," said Kerry said finally.

Ward laughed a little. Kerry turns to him and yelled, "Shut-up."

Aaron said, "Man, dis is gon be intrestin."

The kids took off running over to the well.

"Don't ch'all sticks ya head in dat well," screamed Ressie.

Kerry screamed real low, "Uh-yeah-uh not in da well."

Kat said, "Yes, this is gone be real intrestin."

Ressie sat there with that same look on her face like she was waiting on some kind of confession. We knew that we couldn't talk about anything that might jeopardize who we really were, so we sat there quietly for hours looking around at our new neighborhood. Kids were playing. A few hands, both men and women were standing around talking about the funeral. Some were young and looked like teenagers or young adults in their early twenties. Others were older looking, maybe mid-to-late thirties or early forties. According to history, life expectancy on any plantation rarely went past forty years. They appeared to be not in the best of health. They walked with limps. Some were slightly bent over and I could hear coughing among them. They were all brown-skinned people, only a few were light. I was somewhat able to distinguish those who were seemingly of pure African Ancestry from those who carried the blood of the Europeans. I was both amazed and saddened by this at the same time; a people cut off from who they really were. Gone were their institutes of religion and culture. They were no longer allowed to speak their language. The Africans were physically and mentally destroyed at the hands of a people who based this way of living on their own culture and religious beliefs. I looked at them carrying on business as usual while surviving only on spirit.

Rev surveyed the wooded shacks that seemed to be standing only on faith. There was an outhouse off to the side of the bayou that flowed behind the shacks. He was a long way from his two-story home in the suburbs. There wasn't a limo for him to drive, or a Rolls Royce and definitely not a helicopter or jet that would land and take him away. He just sat there in total disbelief.

Ward seemed to be getting restless. He stood up and said, "Dis is appalling! I can only imagine whad kind of disease I might ketch from da well dat all dese slaves dranks out of and whad about when it's time to use the toilet. I'se ca'nt imagine usin leaves or a cone cob. I'ze has a degree not's ta be around no black stuff like dis! I wanna go home and I demand to go now!"

I stood up quickly while trying to defuse him from loosing it. "Ward! Would you please sit yo scary buhind down and be quiet fo's you say da wrong thang!"

He looked at me with disgust and fear.

"Gone on now," I said.

He surveyed the gang's expression and sensing they were all in agreement with me and, sat down.

Ressie said, "If ya wanna goes home so bad, den gon on, da big house is right de, five minutes unda yo feet."

Ward gave a sigh of relief while swiftly standing and pointing to the mansion. You mean I stays up dere?"

"Yep," Ressie answered. "All yo life madder of fac. You, Kathy and Rev bedda head on up dere now and ansah to you chohs."

Ward glared toward the big house then asked Rev and Kathy, "Whad ch'all waiding on? Let's go. Let's go to da big house."

The others seemed surprised at Ward's sudden change of mood, but I was'nt. The thought of being up at the house in all this madness gave Ward hope of getting back home. I watched Rev and Kat as they hesitantly rose from the bench. Rev nodded his head to affirm Ressie's suggestion.

He said, "Well, John use wuz baptized in my awms as a child, became a man, and neva came back to churt when use got dat job. Neva really heard a word from you since ya tolds me ya graduated from da churt, but I guess I'm gon half ta trust use any hows on dis here."

I shook his hand. "Wees were two men who got lost and separated from our community. Wees both got fat in our own ways. I'se acks God ta bring me back and he did. I'se thank is time fo you to acks him to do da same."

"Maybe so," said Rev, "Maybe so."

Kat then tiptoed up, kissed me on my cheek and started to cry. "John, I am so scayed! I jus don't know if I'm gon make it."

"Don't worry girl," I answered. "If is one thang dat I'se know, is use a strong survivor."

Kathy still crying, "Use knows I ain't strong John. "And evabody knows you don't hangout wit no weak peoples." She began to dry her tears.

"Well, wees hangin out now. Just be strong. I'se aint far from ya and Rev gon be right dere in da same house." I hugged her, while Rev patted her on the back in a show of support. "Now looka yonder at dat fool," referring to Ward whom apparently had gotten over anxious and took off towards the house.

"Maybe he thank the ansah is somewhere in dat big house?" asked Lizzy.

"Naw, he just happy dat he ain't stayin in da qwadas wit da rest of us," Aaron said.

Ressie was checking all of this out listening sharply and carefully to the conversation.

She then tells Rev, "Good evening, Rev. See ya here in da mawning fa churt. Hope yo surmon is upright.

"Das right!" Rev said, surprisingly remembering. "I'se a preacha here."

"You is whadeva Massa Peterson says use is. He taught cha how to preach, so you is a precha," Ressie added.

Rev seemed a little relieved. I told him to keep his eyes and ears open for any clue as to what was going on, but do not explain to anyone. He agreed. Maybe he felt he had a little ammunition to go on. He and Kat started towards the back of the big house. The rest of the gang watched as they faded down the road, which separated the picturesque cotton fields that lead to the back entrance of the house. A group of young ladies strolled by the table and spoke. Some of them had attended the funeral.

"Hows you feelin, Lizzy?" asked one lady.

Lizzy was startled and surprised by the concern of the woman and the fact she knew her name.

She replied, "Fine ya'll, jus fine."

"Good," the lady said. "Wees bes be gon in now."

Ressie picked up on Lizzy's unawareness of what the lady was talking about and stepped in for her.

"It's time fo you to go to da women folks qwadas Lizzy," she said. "Now gon on and get cha self a good nite's sleep, ya hears?"

Lizzy got up and said, "Yes mam; good night ya'll." She looked at me.

"Night Lizzy. Don't fo get to say yo prayers." I said.

"I sho am. Gon pray dat chu no whad chu doing."

As Lizzy walked away with the ladies, we noticed a woman walking in our direction.

"Man-o-man, would ja look at dat," Aaron said.

"Who is dis Fox coming dis way?" I added.

"I don't no, but she sho is nice!" said Kerry.

The lady who was coming our way walked gracefully with both hands folded together in front of her. She was a tall and slender woman with broad shoulders. Her skin was evenly toned, rich in melanin. Her eyes were dark and her hair was natural. It was a blessing to see such a beautiful black woman who had not identified with a hot-comb, perm, wig, weave or any chemical assistance. The three of us were awestruck. We looked like freshman high schoolers gawking at the senior cheerleader.

Ressie said, Das Lila," looking very puzzled. "Das yo wife and da moma of you three chiluns, boy!"

We now knew that the lady who could make any model agency wealthy was the wife of Kerry. She reached the table and smiled at him.

"Husband," she said softly, as if she wasn't sure.

"Huh?" replied Kerry. "I mean mam, no I mean yes-uh-yes, wife," Kerry stumbled. He was so high from her radiance; his feet did not appear to touch the ground.

"Is use okay?" asked Lila. "I'se been worried bout ya but Miss Ressie said you wuz gon be fine."

"Yeah, I'se fine Lila," said an embarrassed Kerry. He was clearly intimidated by the woman who was nearly tall enough to look him in the eye.

"Husband yo supa is gon get cold and Iris wants ta know where huh pappy at," Lila said with concern.

Kerry briefly looked away from Lila, turning to Aaron, Ressie and myself with some confusion. "Good nite ya'll." He said.

Lila reached for his hand. Kerry didn't hesitate to oblige at his wife's request. As the two began to walk off Kerry quickly glanced back at us with a smile. It was as if he was feeling a bit of peace. I hoped he would be okay and handle his situation like a father and husband truly would.

We began to see men heading into the cabins. I asked Ressie, "Guess it's bout time to run in fo da nite?"

Aaron said, "but I'se ai'nt sleepy. Shoot, I'se use to stayin up all night long and hangin out."

I said, "Dis here aint no time to re-live wha'cha use ta doin."

"John's right baby, you just follow dat man wit dat grey shirt on," Ressie said. "Beside don't no black man hangs out afta dawk anywhere dat I know of."

Aaron said, "All right. Goodnight Miss Ressie, John."

I shook his hand as if we were on a night out on Martin

Luther King Blvd. "Hey man member you ain't no stranger to nobody rounds hear so be careful hows you talk now, you hear?"

"Okay John," he said. "At lease I'se wit da field hands! Huh John?"

"Das right my brudder," assuring him of the strength it took to be a field hand. He ran off to catch up with the man and the rest of the men folk.

I looked up at the sky. It was now dark. The sun had faded and I remembered it was daylight savings time. I admired the beauty of the constellation. Looking up at it reminded me of the days we stargazed as kids on the bayou. Starring straight up - nothing seemed any different. I couldn't help but marvel.

I said to Ressie, "aint de jus beautiful?" She gave no reply. When I looked down to see why she had not answered, the expression on her face could have knocked me back. Instead it just scared the hell out of me.

"Why use lookin at me like dat?" I asked.

She peeped to the left and right to see if anyone was near-by, then her dark eyes began to focus on mine as if she could see straight through me. I knew she had something very heavy to tell me and I grew anxious to hear.

"Is dere sumpin you wanna say?" I asked.

She calmly directed me to sit down with her hand. She reached over, picked up my hand and placed it over hers. She leaned forward with those piercing eyes, much like Miss Imani's back home.

"I knows whose ya is," she said, whispering to not arouse any suspicion.

"And jus whose am I?" I said, fearing somehow my identity had been discovered.

"Dat ole oak tree told me who; das why I waded fo ya'll."

I was somewhat relieved after hearing Ressie say this, because if she heard it from an oak tree, she really didn't know who the gang and I really were. There was no way she could know or handle the truth.

She continued, "Use know I ain't no fool John so whad I fen to tell ya won't surprise ya too much. Ya see dat ole oak tree told me dat eva tang round here gon come to past and dat use is da one das gon make sho it does. And da one things dat I'se know is dat oak tree ain't neva lied to me or nare wona my sista's eder. So whad eva use acks me, no madder how crazy it may be, I'se knows use acksin me fo a reason."

"What reason is dat gon be?" I inquired.

"Fo da same reason dose six peoples (referring to the gang) been lookin at'cha like you da king or sumpin. Deys ain't neva looks at cha like dat befo."

I began to reply, but she cut me off holding up her finger and placing it on my lips.

"No-no," she said, "now ain't da time. Ta-marow mawning afta churt use meet me down unda da oak tree. Dat way I'se know if eva thang gon be alright and all da trut gon be told." She stood up using the table as a crutch to help her. I jumped up immediately to assist.

"Now, it's late and Massa's henchman Caleb gon ride through to make sho evabody is in da houses," Ressie said.

I looked at Ressie with the face of a child who had a thousand questions. I got ready to speak again, thinking I could at least inquire about something, but again she cut me off as if she knew I was going to speak.

"Ahp-ahp now," she said, as she put her hand on my jaw I felt the roughness from years picking cotton and tending to the chores of slave life. Her hands were like sandpaper, but somehow gentle and comforting. She looked me in the eyes and smiled.

"Use got yo mama's eyez. All dawk and strong but kind jus like huhs. Dat is so wunderful."

I kissed her on her forehead. "Good nite Miss Ressie."

"Good nite baby. Get cha rest nare ya hear. Ta-mara is Sunday, heh-heh-heh. Yes sur. Ta-mara is aw day," she said as she walked slowly to her house.

I stood there and watched as her frame faded into one of the broken-down houses. There were just no words to describe the pain I felt seeing my people in these conditions. I raised my head back up to the sky hoping it would again help me to forget what was around me. The night air was very cool as the breeze of fall echoed through the trees. The moon was full and every star and planet that God had created seemed to be present. I continued to stare as if the answer to all of this would somehow find its way down to rescue us from the hell we were about to encounter. Suddenly, I heard the sound of horses approaching from the distance. I ran towards the house where Aaron was, pulled back the wool blanket and entered the one-room quarter that was home for the night.

I called out for Aaron very quietly. "Aaron is you woke?"

"Das you John?" asked Aaron.

"Yeah is me. Bes be quiet fo a second." We sat still as the sound of a horse passed through the quarters. I began to view my new home. Beside the room being nearly dark - it was cool and drafty. A small fire burning in the old cast iron potbelly stove kept the shack from being completely cold and totally dark. There were four beds; two were empty, the others occupied. I knew for sure that Aaron was lying in one bed. I didn't know the other, but whomever it was, needed to be treated with caution. The sound of the horse faded in the distance.

"It's OK Aaron." "De gon now," I said.

Aaron sat up and began, "Hey man, o'l Zeke and I has been in here jus talking bout how far long he done came wit his reading," coyly pointing at the figure in the bed. Use member how much ole Zeke wants to know how to read."

"Hey John, heard ya'll took Moma Raylene's funera kinda hard?" Zeke said as he arose from the bed.

I was hesitant to answer, "I'se okay Zeke." It then dawned on me that I was actually conversing with a slave and getting ready to spend the night in slave quarters.

"Kathy stole dis book here a couple of weeks ago from da big house, and I'se been teaching him da words," Aaron said.

"Well," I said, "Dats jus great Zeke. Hopes ya can keeps up da good wuk."

"I'se figa long as ol Aaron's round and Massa don't finds out, I'se guess I be alright," said Zeke. "Well, guess I bedder turn in, tamara's Sunday, aw day. Night chall."

"Night Zeke," Aaron replied.

Unsure and very slowly "I said nite Zeke."

I watched Zeke curl up into a fetal position. The cotton blanket didn't seem like it was going to be enough to cover him but I knew this was just the way it was.

"Man," Aaron whispered, "is dis really happnin? Dis is Sadday nite. Me and my homeboys should be hittin da fawdy's and da clubs."

"Well," I said, "Not dis Sadday night. But I'se tell ya Aaron. I sho hope dis is da only Sadday night you miss."

"Sho hope dat come true. Nite John," he said.

"Nite Aaron,"

I lay there on my side gazing into the small holes of the wood-burning stove. I thought back to the townhouse I had in Augustus Hill and how I use to entertain with my fireplace burning. I thought how far I had come with the knowledge I'd obtained; knowing our African history of slavery and whether finding out about the Peterson family was really worth telling. I mean all the headaches gained from fighting the battles for black people, the injustices of our civil rights. Fighting for a community of African people who continue to rob and kill each other, rape their women, curse their mothers and fathers and abandon their children; a black nation of jealous backbiters who have substituted praising God for cars, clothes, sex, and money. No longer are we sisters and brothers, but bitches and ho's and niggers and fools. Lord, I should just get out of this bed and run till I die. Horus, if there ever was a time I thought about loosing it this was it. But, as I laid there looking into the fire, I began to reflect on what I had studied about all the slaves who had led revolts and how scared they must have been. The brave ones with the odds stacked heavenly against them relying only on the strength of God, like Nat Turner, the Baptist minister.

I began to pray, "Oh Mighty Creator, give me the strength to help my people and give them the understanding that they are humans . I know I can't save all of them here or in the future, but give me the patience and wisdom to do as much for you as you let me, Ashe."

The fire dimmed as I started to worry about the others. Man, this was crazy, me worrying about Sambos. I tried to fall asleep praying that when I awakened all this would have been a bad nightmare. I listened to the sound of an owl echoing the messages from the spirit world through the quarters while crickets began to sing.

The sun barely peeped over the majestic trees on the East side of the plantation, there a rooster perched on a pine log fence around the hog pen, took site of it and screamed that famous screech.

A few hands were already up and about. Today was Sunday the only day according to history that some of the slaves could have off. Sunday became the only sign of humanity during this time. Remembering how religion played it's role in slavery. Some slave-owners played the Christian role by showing the slaves they had compassion. This day was always special with the slaves. It was their day to give thanks to God for letting them that wanted to, live another week and to have this special time set-aside for prayer, good food, and socializing with each other in the midst of all this madness.

Lizzy walked past our house and yelled, "Hey ya'll it's time to get up."

Aaron and Zeke stepped over to the doorway. "Brudder, da't dere is one fine woman," Zeke said referring to Lizzy. "I'se show been want'un ta call on huh." They both walked out to catch up with Lizzy and the other women.

I sat up on the edge of what was supposed to be the bed that I had not really slept in. The rays of the soft morning sun found their way through the numerous holes in the wall and roof of the little house. I could now see things that I couldn't last night. There were no windows. The beds were just boards sitting on tree stumps. There was no table, or chairs. On the far side of the room was a long board that resembled a shelf, which held what looked like a change of field clothes. Under the long shelf was a shorter one that housed soap, grease, salt, pepper, tin cups, and a bucket. There was also a steel washtub. I remembered a tub just like this when I was a kid at my grandmother's in the country. I went over to the bucket hoping that it contained water, it did. I dipped my hands into it splashing water on my face. There was no towel to dry so I used my shirt. I used a tin cup to get water and rinse my mouth. There would be no mouthwash today.

Just then a voice yelled out, "John?" It was Ressie.

I stepped out the door. "Good mawnin, Miss Ressie."

She said, "Come on baby, let's gon ova here and see what Masa done told Rev to tell us dis time."

As we began to walk to the clearing at the end I saw Kerry and his new family. He and Lila were walking side by side. Iris was getting a ride on his back while his two sons kicked rocks a couple of feet in front of them. As we reached the last house on the right Rev was there to greet everyone as they walked up. It hadn't crossed my mind, but I realized now why this house was larger than any other. It was reserved as a house of worship. A wooden crucifix was over the door. As we walked in, Rev spoke and couldn't help but give me a wink, he knew I didn't attend church. The room was filled with slaves sitting on benches very quietly. Only a few voices could be heard. A podium was up front for Rev to lean on with a big picture of the European version of our Lord and Savior behind it.

Rev came in after the last slaves arrived standing behind the podium he said, "Mawin evabody!"

"Mawnin Rev!" the hands replied.

"Fo we get stawded, wees gon sang a song to da lawd" Rev said, turning briefly to the portrait of the blond-haired man. "Dis song is called, "Wash me Lawd, Wash me White as Snow."

I bowed my head, placed my fingers over my left eye, and shook my head in disgust. There was no way. I would sing this song, not in 1831, 1931, or 2031; no way in hell. Rev raised his hands, palms up, gesturing for us to stand. As everyone stood, I remained seated. Ressie reached for my hand to stand. I knew I had to because Ressie wanted me to, but I convinced myself it was probably better to do so than draw attention. I had heard the song before when I attended church in Augustus Hills. I was unconscious in those days. It never bothered me when I joined in with the choir. I listened to the hands singing. None of the gang appeared to know the words, but Ward. His head was moving from side to side with every word that he sang, as if almighty God would personally see to it that he be washed. After the song, Rev motioned for us to sit, then pulled out some notes from a Bible he had gotten from Master Peterson. According to history this was how it was done. He began to preach in accord with the notes.

"The servant is to obey his Masta. Our work here on earth is for suffrin. Da trials and tribulations we goes through heps us earn our ree-ward in heaven," Rev said, pointing to the sky. He then picked up the Bible.

"Wees gots ta believe in dis here book. Da wuds tells us to be humble and lovnin like da lamb who is Jesus Christ!" He shouts turning and glancing at the picture.

The slaves all respond, "Yes Sur, Aman"

Rev continued, "Use see? Wees can't hate Massa Peterson, naw-naw. Das wrong! Wees got ta love and fogive Massa, cause da lawd said fo give him fo he not know what he do! Can I get a Aman?" He shouted so the slaves could feel the emotion of the message Massa had given him to speak.

I nearly became sick to my stomach. Ressie saw the look on my face. She sat there with me, not singing the song and appeared to be paying no attention to Rev.

"Hang in dere, baby," she said with a smile while squeezing my hand.

Rev continued but I tuned him out. I knew he had to be convincing. It was just in him to do so; he collected no tithes and gave no message to the people about getting the "things" that he had gotten through faith in God. I began to reflect on the evolution of the black church, from the time of Absalom Jones, Richard Allen and the establishment of the African Methodist Church. A church that was established to support abolitionists and teach collective organization and liberation through the Underground Railroad and revolts. Rev's message this morning however also exists in modern times. The sad thing is that many people still believe it. Studying African history, I found out that before we stepped off the boat into slavery and were introduced to the European form of Christianity, using the King James Version, African people were doing fine with their spirituality. As I felt Ressie next to me I thought of how her and Miss Imani's strength reflected the kind of strength it took Rosa Parks to make a stand, the kind of spirit that women had throughout the villages of our West African homeland. You see, the woman was the head of many of our religious practices. She was our preacher, but since arriving in America we've been taught differently. Maybe, that's why male chauvinism and sexism prevail in many of our churches.

Rev announced that service was over and to bow our heads as he prayed. He then dismissed service and walked to the door to shake hands with his congregation. As we headed out, Ressie said, "Go on and meet cha peoples and sees how de doing. I'se gon meetcha back down unda de ol oak tree. I godda go have my churt now heh-heh-heh," she laughed.

I walked out the church and waited for the gang to come out while motioning them over to the table. It was still not quite noon yet Rev was the last to come to the table. He shook hands with the church members; still speaking, giving blessings and hope.

Aaron asked, "Kinda funny giving free advice? Huh, Rev? I'se bet use neva gave a free surmon."

Rev looked angrily at Aaron "When I'se won me a gospal awad, I'se thank God fo givin me wuds to help people. When you won a awad, use thank God fo call'in peoples bitches and niggahs. Whose do you thank is in trouble?"

Aaron jumped up immediately to go after Rev. Kerry and I quickly intervened. Aaron yelled, "You da biggest pimp in da hood!"

Some of the hands turned around. "Ya'll stop," I said, trying not to be too loud.

"Man, yo ass gots ta chill," Kerry angrily said to Aaron.

"Whad kinda chances ya'll two thanks we gon have of gettin oudda here, if dis da way we gon ack? And Rev, if you stawd cussin we sho in trouble," I said.

Rev replied, "Well I'se still a man and I don't like been disrespected about who I am."

"Neder do I!" Aaron said as he sat back down.

"Boys, boys", Lizzy said, "Can ya'll leave da macho stuff alone till weze get back."

"I know das right," Kat added.

We sat down taking a few seconds and a deep breath to calm the moment.

I asked how everybody was doing. Rev appeared to have calmed from the confrontation, so I started with him.

"How'd evathang go last nite? Did ja see aw here anythang that coulda been a clue fo us?"

"Not really, John," answered Rev. "Da white folks up dere don't have no physical contact witcha. We had to weah white glove survin dem and all."

"Das right, John," Kathy said. "Dey don't say nudin to ya and de don't want cha round em unless deys tell ya."

"How many white folks is it?" I asked.

"Can't say fo sho, answered Rev. "Dere's old man Ugusta..."

Lizzy interrupted, "Ain't he da one dat stawded all of dis. Dat da street and dose townhomes name afta?"

"Yeah, he da one," I said.

Rev continued, "His wife and him has two chilun. A son named Claude and a nudda son dat I'se not seen name Bobby."

"Well, keeps ya eyes and eah's open Rev," I said, "How's you ladies holding up?"

"I didn't sleep a wink," Kat said. "I'se neva been dis scayed in my life. I seen my face in a mirah dis mawning and scayed myself. I jus cried and cried. One of da ladies dat was in de room wit me figa I'se still cryin bout Moma Raylene. I'm gon try hawd ta be strong but I'm not gon make no promises."

"Jus hang on Kat. Best use stay as close to dose udder house ladies," I told her, "How's bout you Lizzy?"

"Jus like Kat I didn't sleep a'tall," Lizzy said "Dat board I was layin on was hawd. I prayed a lot fo strength, and I realize dis ain't no dream. But, I'se gots to be honest wit ya'll, I'm scayed. I can't eva member a time when I couldn't find an ansah to my problem."

We all felt the fear the ladies had expressed. I told them to continue to pray for strength and a way out. I turned to Aaron for his account of the night and I tried to break some tension.

"Aaron, I'se know dat use okay by da way use snowin," I said. He grinned a little like the others bowing his head.

"I jus prayed like eva one else, I guess? Been awhile since I done dat," Aaron said.

Rev added with a low-keyed voice "Das alwys a good way to go you know."

In that moment he and Aaron made eye contact. The expression on Aaron's face seemed apologetic to the man who had baptized him as a baby. I then turned to Kerry and kept my campaign up easing tension.

"Hey famly man!" I said smiling, "ya'll look mighty nice in churt dis mawin."

Kerry had a look that was somewhat peaceful he seemed to be suspended in thought.

"Kerry? Uth (earth) to-Kerry," I said.

He blurted out as if he had been in a zone of some kind, "Man! I. jus cai'nt splane how it felt to lay next to a woman and not thank uhbout havin sex wit huh. I mean she is so soft but she feels strong. Not like she got muscles or anythang but her attitude is all for me. She makes me feel like I'se needs to go out and do sumpin fo huh and dose kids, man. Dose kids jus stahs (stares) at me like de cai'nt du nudding less I'se tell em I mean dey not bad or nudding, but..."

Kerry who had his head halfway down while he was talking now looked up at the group who was listening with shock on their faces.

Now why is ya'll lookin at me like dat? He said.

My face was numb; the nerves in it must have stopped. Both Ward and Rev's mouths were half-opened, heads hanging down but still able to see this NBA superstar. Lizzy was smiling shaking her head. Kathy put one hand over her mouth and the other was raised up signaling stop as if she was a crossing guard for kids. Aaron put both his hands on the top of his head and looked at Kerry in utter disbelief.

"Man! Whad da hell done happen ova nite to you."

"Alright!" said Lizzy, "Girlfriend gots game."

She reached over to Kat and gave her a high-five who replied, "Use go gul," referring to Lila.

"Boy dat gul done put sumpin in you tayta pie," said Rev.

Kerry defended himself like an embarrassed kid whose secret crush on his teacher had been revealed. "All ya'll be quet." I'm just saying she ain't like no udda woman I done met be-fo das all. I'se mean we ain't done nuddin."

"Not yet anyway," said Ward.

Aaron said, "Man use wupped an ain't even got dat."

I stopped Aaron short of finishing his sentence. "Hey! Dat's enough ya'll." But I couldn't resist a poke at him. "Boy dat Lila got some juju huh?"

Kerry looked puzzled, "Whas dat?"

"Neva mind," I replied.

Kerry didn't say anything else. He just seemed frustrated. I told him that even though he had mixed feelings the experience was okay and definitely good for him. It was now Ward's time to give his account. I must admit it was good to see the gang relieve some tension but I knew it could all change with what Ward could say. I was reluctant to believe anything he might add yet I knew I had to show him that he was a part of the group.

Ward began, "I'se still very shook up bout all of dis. I don't has a mind fo all of dis. It just scays me ta det, but if da women can make it, I can too."

I nodded my head affirmatively to let him know I understood. "Das good Ward. Membahs ta keep ya eyes and eahs open. Naw ya'll listin up. Taday is Sundey, and dere ain't no wuk. But we mus all keeps aw eyes and eahs open fo anythang that may be a clue to get home. Naw ya'll mus membah ya'll got lives here be-fo wees arrived. Na-uh I knows dat sounds crazy, but last night Aaron and I met a man name Zeke who said dat Kat had stole a book fo him weeks ago."

The puzzled gang starred at each other. Beginning to feel that this was real, one hundred percent and that their answers would come if they begin to observe and assimilate into this environment.

"So's we jus goes on and till I'se figa out whad we gon do next. Again, I godda emphasize dese black folk here knows ya'll as udda hands. Don't go talkin to dem like deys folk whose goes to da same malls as ya'll do, or yell's fo da Lakers, ya here?"

They all agreed with a nod and few yeah's but Ward seemed to be agitated so I asked, "Is dere sumpin you wanna say Ward?"

"Yeah, I'se got a question fo ya," said Ward. "Who done put you in chawge?"

I stood up, as did he. We were face to face but no one intervened. I knew it would come to this sooner or later.

"Don't cha know by now, Wawd?" I asked.

He answered, "Knows I don't, Mr. Af-free-ca!"

"Aw ancesta's did," I said passionately. And for whateva reason ya'all don't believe dat I'se sorry but their spirits are alive and I believe dat de are maybe trying to use us for sumpin.

I knew I had mentioned this to the gang when we arrived at the cemetery. It was a subject that they couldn't handle but I had to plant a seed in their heads to get them to think about how we may have gotten here and how this may be the only way we leave.

I continued at Ward. "So if use got a problem wit dat den use convince me and da res of us dat, yo Sambo ass know whad da hell to do, huh?"

I starred him down. He turned to see the others, hoping someone would step up on his behalf, but the expression on their faces were in anticipation of him giving an answer better than mine. Ward gave us his answer by lowering his head and sitting down.

"Na-uh let's all go on and make da bes of dis heer day. I has ta talk to Miss Ressie but we bes meets back hear fo sundown."

Ward jumped up and stormed away. As he headed down the trail that led to the rear of the big house, I told the group, "Wit all da knowledge my ancestas done gave me, none of ya'll trust dat brudder, not one bit."

"Hey John," said Kerry. "Whad is a Sambo?"

"Watching Ward head down the trial, I said, "He jus lef da table."

I headed for the old oak tree to meet Ressie. I took the path that the gang and I had discovered yesterday. It appeared to be afternoon, but I didn't know the exact time. As I walked by the cotton fields to my left, I couldn't help but be captivated by this plant that seemed synonymous with slavery. It resembled a million snowflakes that had fallen on a field of tall grass and remained there to be marveled. To my right were endless rows of corn that swayed widely in all directions, their long stems dancing to the rhythm of the wind. It was a splendor to see all this, but sad to think of the institution that it had created.

I neared the oak tree and saw Ressie sitting patiently on a block of wood apparently cut out of a large tree trunk.

"Aftanoon, Miss Ressie. How's ya doing?" I asked.

"Fine baby, jus fine. Haf a seat rit-chea," she said, pointing down to the ground beside her. "I needs you to open yo eahs up, cuz whad I'se bout to tell ya is why evathang is da way it is, but fust you must po some of dis here wader on the ground, on yo head, then drink the rest."

She handed me the cup of water and I did the ritual. She put her hand on my head. As a strange but gentle wind blew, I was slightly knocked off balanced. A cold haunting breeze came; the same one I felt back at the ceremony when the black cloud appeared. The wind closed my eyes as the music of the oak tree played a rustling song. The chimes hanging from a branch above rang quietly. I could feel the water flow through me. I wondered if she had put something in it.

"Deys here," said Ressie.

"Who?" I asked confusingly.

"You knows," she said.

"Da ancestas? Huh? Da ancestas has come?" I said nervously.

Ressie answered, "Das right baby, deys all here."

The wind calmed. Anticipation was under the oak tree. Ressie stared out into the fields like she was in a trance, a spiritual zone. She began to speak. "I'se came heer wit my sista's Paulene and Raylene from Naw'lins over twenty yeas ago. Massa Ugusta Peterson bought us from a shuga plantation own by a man name Tib-aw-doe. Reason bein is dat he hads no women folks here. Da men folks build de house and we guls built da fields fo five aw six yeas. Massa Ugustas wife, Miss Ruth, taut us hows we spose to ack and whad wees spose to do. Wees only chilun's. But wees learn fast. Puddy soon wees told it was time to make younguns. Massa Ugusta told's us whose we ta be wit. Didn't madder if we like'em or not. I wuz da younges of da tree of us so I'se told to wait a year. Yo moma wuz Paulene. She wuz da oldes and Raylene wuz da midda child. Da man dat had Raylene wuz from da homland. Das how's Lizzy gots here. Das whys she so dawk and puddy. Den came all da mess. Massa Ugusta stawded makin mo money off aw wuk and moved up in da wul. So, Miss Ruth becames a lady. He stawds to make rides out to da qwades at night to see Raylene. Das whez Ward and Kathy comes from. Lizzy's pappy wuz cleen run off from heer. Das da main reason de's be wukin in da house now. Cuz dey belongs to Ugusta. Den Massa figas he mite as well has his way wit Paulene too cuz de hand she wuz spose to be wit had hawd times makin younguns."

Ressie reached over and grabbed my hand. She had never stopped starring at the fields. The look on her face was frozen. Nothing moved except her lips and an occasional blink of the eye. She squeezed my hand as I moved suddenly like something had jumped inside of me. My head bowed over, I raised it up and stared out into the fields just like Ressie.

She continued, "Massa Peterson rode out heer to da qwadas one night fo Paulene but he drunk so much of dat moonshine he fell off his hoss. Rev took um back to da big house. His boys, young Claude and his lil brudder Bobby, gots full of his moonshine and rode into de qwadas. De came across Paulene and huh man. Claude pulled a shotgun out an tolds da man dat he would kill'em if he tried to stop dem frum takin and havin de way with huh. Dat ol man had been broken like a wild ol hoss anyhows so it didn't take much fo Claude and Bobby to scay him. De took Paulene down to da ba-yo. Bobby helds huh down while Claude had his way wit huh. She fought fo a bit but de wuz too strong.

I jumped up in anger. "Dat sorre son of a bitch."

Ressie said, "Sit down baby. Geddin mad at sumpin you cai'nt change cai'nt heps ya. Now go on an sits down."

Ressie was very calm despite my expression of anger. She said, "Dare is mo fo me to tells ya."

As I sat there she put her hand on my shoulder with pressure "Claude is yo pappy."

I grabbed my head with both my hands while bowing down with anger and disgust. I knew all along from my coarse but straight hair, my knowledge of history during these times, that many African people were mixed with the blood of their European oppressors. I just believed that never knowing was the safest way to be. I had even claimed some of my ancestry to be Native Americans to save face. But after hearing from Ressie who had no reason to lie I couldn't help but feel disappointed.

She asked, "Use gon be okay baby?"

"Yeah," I said roughly. "Go on and finish."

"Yo moma, Paulene, neva got ova howz you came to be. When use wuz ol enough to wuk Massa threaten to sell ya away. So yo moma, who by this time had taken Aaron in afta Massa bought him and gaves him ta huh ta raise up figas she would run away nawth to gon finds da boat dat takes ya back to Af-free-ca. It wuz a day kinda like tadey. Yo mama waded fo sundown and tooks you and lil Aaron. She runs about fi miles nawth fo Massa Claude, Bobby and dat hench-man of dere's, Caleb finds huh.

"Howd de find huh?" I asked curiously.

"Dat young fool Ward had ova heard sum of us talkin and went back an tolds his pappy, Massa Ugusta." Even as a small boy Ward wuz no good.

I shook my head, "I reckun I'se shoud'nt be surprised."

Ressie continued, "When de brawd huh back here dat nex mawing, de brung us all out to da clearin. Dey tied huh to da two wuppin poles. Massa Ugustus and his boys was all lookin from hossback. Den Massa Claude looked at his pappy. He got a okay look from him and tells dat Caleb to do it. Dat ol Caleb musta bee-cho moma fo awile. Massa Ugusta had been acksin Paulene to beg but she wouldn't do it. So he tells Caleb to hole on while Claude got off his hoss and went ova to Paulene. He stared huh right in da eyes an tells huh to beg fo mercy in front of his family aw dat he would hang huh fo sho. When Claude said dat it sent cold chills down da back of eva hand dat wuz listnin. He and dat Caleb is da two meanes men alive ya know? Jus den, yo moma raised huh head up and looked at Claude. Knealin on huh knees she said to him dat as long as she wuz alive she wuz gon run and dat his family wud'nt neva gon be able to sleep. Dat it be de bes intres ta kill huh cuz she neva gon bow down to his fam-ily. She said dat she hoped dey pu-uh white skin buns in hell. Claude had a look dat wud'nt nuddin but da devil. He den kicked yo moma in da face. Eva hand on da grounds, house and field saw it. Dere wuz not a dry eye standing. All ya'll chill'un saw it too," Ressie said, breathing a sigh.

I was in the spirit. All of this Ressie had been saying was in my head, very clear and detailed. Tears streamed down my stone straight face somehow making it out the corners of my closed eyes. I was motionless, hurt, angry, and said nothing. My tongue was locked but my mind was open.

Feeling my pain Ressie started again, "Das da way eva man, woman and child felt at dat time. Massa Ugusta knowed den he had ta kill Paulene. Ya see, wud came down from Vah-gen-ya and Cal-lina dat slaves had been gon on whad de call uprisins, breakin out and running through da fawms and da fields, bunin and killin white folks and dey chilluns too. Some of da slaves dey caught was prechas dat said God tol'um to do it."

Ressie had'nt realized, but she was telling me history I had read. The slave revolts were the product of spirited African people who could not live plantation life. The willingness to risk their lives, fighting their oppressor, or running from him was always an extraordinary event to read about. The slave revolts, most notably the Reverend Nathaniel "Nat" Turner's, was one of the vehicles that some politicians used in that time to push for the abolishment of slavery. I also knew that beating a slave in front of all the others, especially the children, sent such a powerful message about breaking any of the master's rules on the plantation; that message is still being sent today in other forms by policemen, politicians, and some bosses in the workplace.

Ressie continued, "Claude told Caleb ta untie yo moma and brings huh to dis ol oak tree here. Den tells all da hands to gon back ta wuk sept da chilluns. He tells Rev ta load'em all up in da wagon and hauls'em down to dis tree. Massa Ugusta jus smiled, told Claude, "Das da wayz ta handal biddness. Den he rode off to da big house. All dose young'uns rode down dere scayed ta det. Dere wuz no dry-eye on da wagon, not even Rev. Caleb brought yo moma ova here. Raylene and I tried to stop him but he hit Raylene so hard she passed out. Bobby grabbed me while Caleb throwed Paulene ova his hoss. He is da meanest Af-free-can dere is. De bought huh to dis block I'se sittin on. Da chi-lluns, Rev, and Claude looked at her. Paulene was cussing Caleb and da whole Peterson family. She even stawded ta talk de talk of de ol cunchre. She den said, "Ah-free-ca," ova and ova. It stawded scaying Claude. He den told Caleb to kick dis heer block an dat wuz it. Caleb got back on his hoss and rode off wit Massa Claude. Rev and da kids jus sat dere cryin and hollin while wachin huh slowly turn wit da wind. Raylene and I ran all da way down dere, wees cryin and hollin too. Wees got huh down somehow. I'se don't quite member jus hows. We put huh on da wagon and made Rev walk back wit da young'uns. De had seens mo dan any young'uns should see. But, da stranges thang wuz seein dat you jus sat dere in da wagon. Dere was no tears in yo eyes. Raylene looked at cha like she saw sumpin. She den told Rev ta leaves you wit us. We den took Paulene up to da cemetery and gave huh back to God in da Ah-fee-con way to gon be with de Ancestas."

Ressie dropped her head and let out a deep breath and I opened my eyes at the same time, they were still misty. Life found its way back into my face. I turned to Ressie and stood after helping her to stand up. I gave her a hug and started to cry. She patted me with her strong and gentle hand placing it in the middle of my back. She was unsuccessful at raising her hand any higher against my tall body. I draped over the thin-framed woman now knowing who she was. The images of pain and suffering from people of African descent ran through my head. I thought of the invasion of the Nile Valley otherwise known as the Garden of Eden; the slave dungeons of Ghana and the "Door of no Return," the breaking up of families on the auction blocks; the confrontations of the Knight Riders, the deaths of those in the fifties and sixties.

And I thought how tragically and brutally my ancestral mother, Paulene, had died. I let go of Ressie. Still fighting back my emotions, I stopped crying as we each sat back down.

I just shook my head. "Das some pow-ful story," I said.

"Das how da trut wuks when aw ancesta's da one giving it," Ressie said.

I again starred into the fields, rethinking the story and thinking how the gang and I were all connected. Ressie was quiet, gazing at the rows of corn swaying back and forth sadly humming a tune. I knew now that Ressie and Raylene were my aunts, Paulene my mother, and Claude was my father. Elizabeth was the daughter of Raylene and an African. She then gave birth to Kathy and Ward for Augustus Peterson, which explained why they were fair skinned and worked in the house. It was mind blowing to think that Lizzy, Ward and Kathy were brothers and sisters. And what was even more astonishing was that Kathy and Ward's big brother, Claude, was my father. Four people all connected but couldn't stand to be in the same room. Aaron and Kerry were purchased to work and breed. Rev was with the Petersons when they first arrived it was amazing to see the metaphysics at work. The same energy that is running now in everyone exists in 1999, but there was still a piece missing. I turned to Ressie.

"Miss Ressie," I said, "howz did my Aunt Raylene die?"

Ressie said, "My sista neva got ova da way Paulen died. Fo yeas she moaned ova huh det until finely she made up huh mind to poisun da whole Peterson family. That was a couple of deys ago. But, dat buzzard Ward, always creepin and peepin, told Massa Claude. Massa Claude made Raylene take da poisun huh self right de in frunt of evabody."

I asked Ressie, "You means Ward not only heps kill my mama, he heps kill his own?"

"Das right," said Ressie, "Madders of fac, we wuz sayin goodbye to huh, when all ya'll stawded to talk crazy."

"One mo question, Miss Ressie." "Who wuz da white man dat wuz threatnen us in da cemetery?"

"Das da man I knows you want ta meet but it be bes baby dat ya watch yo step rounds him," Ressie said.

"Ya mean dat dere man wuz Claude?"

"Yep," answered Ressie. "Now ya knows whez ya come from but dere's sumpin else use gota understand. My moma came straight from da homeland and wuz a u-ro-buh (Yoruba) woman. Das like uh preecha ya know."

I nodded my head that I understood because Miss Imani was also a Yoruba priestess.

Ressie said, "Aw mama tawt us de ways when we wuz younguns in Naw'lins. But she said Raylene wuz special; dat she carried da wuds, eyes, and da souls of aw peoples. Dat mawning fo Raylene died we met unda dis tree. She told me she had talked to da spirits of all da U-ro-buhs (youruba) da night befo and dat she knew it wuz huh last day here. Dat de told huh a boy gon come to be a man and dat all dis kinda plantation life gon come to pass cus of him."

"Is dis whad you wuz tryin to tell me las night afta evabody left da table, Ressie?"

"Das rite John. Use da one dat Raylene wuz talkin bout. She said ta me dat mawning that afta huh body returns to da ground, huh spirit wuld come up again and live in da man. And as soon as weze bured huh at noon Sadday use and dos udders stawd talkin crazy. Tooks me awhile to figa out das why I didn't tells ya da rest tills ya heard whad de ancestas hads to say. Raylene also tells me alot bout da numba seven. It ain't all cleah right now, but I knows its gon come to me."

I was bewildered. I scratched my head, put my hand under my chin and walked around the tree. I starred out into the fields again but this time with strength. According to Ressie, despite my interracial background, I had the blood and spirit of a proud people. I had been selected to lead something here and the gang was involved. Whatever differences I had with the Sambo's needed to be dropped - even with Ward. There was no way I could totally convince them that I was chosen to lead them in some kind of revolt or liberation and that we needed to unify for our freedom and survival; according to Ressie all of this would come to pass. When and how that was going to happen I didn't know but I felt the answer would come just as it came today.

Ressie stood and said, "It's time fo us ta head down to the qwadas."

We started to walk back. I began wondering about something Ressie said. "You mentioned sumpin bout numba seven?"

"Raylene told me dat evathang da spirits let huh know wuz about seven, or seven sumpin? I'se can't member now. I wuz hit puddy hawd when she wuz tellin me bout huh dying. But I'se go pray dat it comes back to me, okay baby?" said Ressie.

"Das fine, Miss Ressie," I answered.

Chapter IV

LET'S MAKE A SLAVE

As Ressie and I approached the cabins the smell of food overtook the air. The sound of hands clapping, children laughing, men talking loudly and the steady beat of a tambourine echoed through the quarters. It was Sunday the off day for most slaves. As we reached the clearing my thoughts and images of the afternoon with Ressie were taken over by the joyous smiles and the festive moment that we would experience.

In the clearing the hands had formed a circle. Kerry and Lila danced hand and hand like a newly married couple celebrating their reception. Next to them was Zeke smiling like a fox in a hen house as he jumped up and down joyously in front of an embarrassed Lizzy. Other slaves were coupled to help form the circle. Just outside the circle Aaron and Kat were beating rhythmically with tambourines as though they were drums. The kids had also made a circle of their own as older field and house hands sat down at one of the long tables to eat. Kerry's three kids and two other little girls who seemed to have taken a liking to Kat all tugged on her arms and dress knocking her off rhythm. It was amazing to see people find joy at a time that was designed to bring them so much pain.

They screamed "Miss Kad-de (Kathy) we'ze hongry! We'ze hungry!"

She gave the tambourine to another lady and went over to the festive table to prepare plates for the children. It was good to see the gang focusing on something positive to relieve the tension and fear-if only for a while. Next to the table where Kat was preparing plates sat a very disgusted Ward. I thought about whom he was, realizing the only reason he wasn't dead was because he was the son of the master. His arms were folded while watching the slaves dance. He considered them beneath him.

I went over to Kat and put my arm around her. "Hey John!" she said.

"Do ya feels any bedder?" I asked.

"I'se okay fo now," answered Kat.

I added, "Looks like ya got cho hands full."

Kat answered, "Dese two lil guls right here minds me of minds back home." Her eyes beginning to tear.

"Use gon be fine," I said. "I'se got news fo us. Tell da udders to meet here fo sundown."

"Okay John," Kat said.

Just then Rev shouted out "Wade a min it. Dese heer chilluns done already ate once. Hows many times you gon feed em?"

Kat pierced her eyes at the kids like that of an angry mother. Kerry's daughter little Iris said "Uh Oh," as she and the kids got up.

They took off running while heading towards the bayou. They gathered rocks to throw in the water. Rev turned around and got back down to business. The table was covered from one end to the other with the slaves' dinner of soul food. Fresh corn on the cob, cabbage, yams, squash, fried chicken, fresh fried catfish out the bayou and a batch of hot water cornbread were evident! I gazed at the food. Although not having an appetite in all this madness was understandable, I knew I had to eat something to maintain my strength. Besides Horus this is food that our people have been preparing before they came to these shores. The knowledge of preparing these dishes was something I once read in an article.

The vibrant food traditions of not only the American South but also the Caribbean and Central and South America owe much to African foods and the cooking techniques brought to these regions by African slaves. Watermelon, which is thought to have originated in Southern Africa and was harvested in Egypt more than four thousand years ago, and which came over with captives, has become a staple of the American picnic and barbecue. The rice culture that made the fortunes of the Carolina low country and built the mansions on Charleston's battery began when the grain was brought to the North American colonies in the seventeenth century. Blacks from the coast of West Africa used their knowledge of rice cultivation to grow successful crops. Peanuts originated in South America, traveled to Europe and Africa, and later returned to the Western Hemisphere aboard slave ships bound for the United States. There the peanut retained vestiges of its Kimbundu name from Angolo, <u>nguba,</u> which became "goober." In Carolina's low country sesame keeping its name from Senegal's Wolof language is still known as <u>benne</u>.

Once on New World shores, Blacks combined these and other familiar foods with native meats and fish, legumes and vegetables, herbs and spices to create ingenious new cuisines. The word <u>nkruma,</u> from the Twi language in Ghana, became <u>okra</u> or a name for the fuzzy pods that Africans used to thicken soups and stews. The vegetable's Bantu names, <u>tchingombo and quingombo,</u> lent their sonorities to okra-based dishes ranging from New Orleans' gumbo to Brazil's <u>quiabada</u>. Deep-fat frying techniques brought over by people such as the Yoruba from southwest Nigeria inspired dishes like "gospel bird" (fried chicken so named because it was often served in African-American homes after church on Sundays)[1].

I moved to the center of the table where Rev sat and realized why he was in that spot. In the center of the table was a bowl covered by a towel. As Rev reached to pull it back I became nauseous. The bowl contained pig ears, pigtails, pig feet and a whole mess of guts or "chilttlins." I turned to Kat with a bitter frown.

She laughed and said, "Ya wanna plate full don' cha?"

"Yeah!" I said, "eva thang sept dat swine. I ain't gon out like dat."

Rev whose lips and hands were greasy said, "You don't knows wha cha missin John," never raising his head and laughing.

"Yeah right," I replied. Look at cha a hog eatin hog."

Kat put my plate in front of me and I began to eat. The food was quite good. From the chicken to the vegetables the deliciousness of the fresh farm cooked food was great especially the fried bayou catfish. I tried not to eat too much so I could stay alert and save a little room for the sweet potato pie at the end of the table. Most of the older people got up from the table and headed over to the houses that had chairs made out of tree stumps. Others stepped on to a trail that apparently led down to the bayou. The gang and I remained at the table, sharing our company were Lila, Zeke and Ressie. After dinner and dessert we began a hearty ritual of rubbing bellies and picking teeth.

Zeke then asked Lizzy, "I'se be much ah-blige Lizzy if ya joins me in a walk downs by da bahyo." Lizzy appeared as though she had just been asked to go to the prom.

She answered, "Why Zeke, I'se thank I would like dat."

1 Harris Jessica B. Cultural Crossroads. <u>America Legacy</u> Spring 2001 Volume 7/Number 1

Kerry turned to Lila and said, "Hey I'se guess we awda walks some of dis here food off." Lila obliged her husband's request and they too walked on.

Ressie stood and said to Rev, "Well! Mr. Precha. Is yo belly bouts to pop as always?"

"Heh-heh", Rev chuckled. "Fo dat happins I'se gon get you to walks wit me down to da bahyo." He extended his forearm out to Ressie who smiled and took him up on his offer.

"Oh well!" said Kat. "I guess weze awda join da res of um fo wees pop. So come on fellas bes go check on dem chillun's fo de get in trouble."

The trail that led down to the bayou started a little ways outside the quarters. It was a well-walked trail. Obviously along with the ritual Sunday meal it appeared that taking a walk down to the bayou was a big part of the day. I knew Zeke had a crush on Lizzy and it was starting to show as they walked ahead of us on the trail overlooking the bayou on our left. As they talked and laughed with one another I remained cautious. Zeke was not only struck by Lizzy's sharpness, but how strong and smart she was compared to the other women. I hoped Lizzy would remember where we were and not take Zeke's honesty and sincerity the wrong way. This man's conversation would not begin with his car and career. Zeke walked barefoot and was a slave. The men she had known wore fancy suits and flashed their money. Zeke wore torn clothes that were too small and was never given a dime. But by her laughter she was clearly taken by the innocence of this grown man with the mind of a Sunday school kid although his mannerisms and slow accent showed an educational void, he was full of kindness and devotion. Zeke surprisingly took Lizzy's hand as I watched them closely.

Zeke asked Lizzy, "Lizzy, I'se like ta know if I could stawd calling on ya?"

"Wad is you goals and dreams Zeke?" was Lizzy's conditioned response.

Zeke looked at her in confusion, thought for a second as to what Lizzy was asking, then responded in the best way he could.

"Well, Massa Claude says I'se got a real strong back and I'se figa since use got a real strong mind maybe weze can get to gedder one day and jump da broom."

Lizzy stopped in her tracks. I could not have helped what I had overheard, hoping only that Lizzy would remember to be calm, but the frown on her face said otherwise.

"Wad!" she yelled.

"Wees could have some strong an smawt chilluns. Lots of um. Dat uh make da Pedersons reals happy!" added an over-anxious, but nervous Zeke.

"Look Zeke!" yelled Lizzy, her neck rolling around like it was no longer attached to her body. "We ain't fen ta jump no broom an I'se sho ain't fenna have no chilluns for you or da Pedersons!" She walked off hurriedly down the trail as Zeke walked desperately behind her. Kerry and Lila who had also witnessed this turned to us as if we knew what had happened. I was reluctant to say anything so I kept quiet.

"Wad wuz dat all bout?" asked Lila.

"Maybe she gave him da key to huh house back," Kerry said playfully.

Lila looked at him strangely. "Use sho beens talking funny since Mama Raylene's fu-nal. Use sho use all right?"

"I'se fine Lila," Kerry said putting his arm around her.

Lila said, "Ya knows husband dere has been talk dat Massa may sells some of us and get some new hands in here. De says some of da mens das still young an strong may get new women."

Kerry saw the sadness in Lila's eyes. He didn't quite know what to say never having dealt with a situation that even came close to this. His wife waited for an answer. He knew there was no lie he could tell so the truth would have to be told. They both stopped. She put her arms up with her hands resting on his shoulders.

Lila asked, "Husband tell me eva thang gon be all right. Tells me Massa gon leaves us alone. I's wants my family here."

I could tell by the look on Kerry's face that he felt her pain. He turned around to see me eavesdropping. I tried quickly to glance off, but he knew I had heard. Turning back to Lila he tried offering some comfort.

"Hey, calms down now ya here. Ain't no sence in gidden yo self all wuked up for nuddin. I'se and da chilluns ain't gon no whea. Wees gon be right here," Kerry said not really knowing for sure what the outcome could be. All he knew was that for whatever reason this was happening to his wife; the mother of his three kids and us. They loved him unconditionally. He saw something in her that he had never seen in the eyes or the personality of any woman he had ever known.

She kissed and hugged him very tightly as if the master might take him away from her at that moment. Kerry felt the warmth of Lila's passion. The hug transcended a presence to him that she would only be secure and strong if he were in her life. They stood there holding each other. Rev and Ressie walked past me.

"Seen enough?" asked Ressie.

I hadn't realized my curiosity was that obvious. I walked on past the two as though I was trying to catch up with Rev and Ressie. I heard Kerry whisper to Lila. "I'se promise you Lila wees always gon be to gedder."

I couldn't help but feel Kerry was getting caught up in the moment or maybe he really needed a woman like Lila back home. Whatever the case, I knew he was headed for trouble. I walked behind Rev and Ressie. Kat, Aaron, and Ward caught up with me as we all strolled down the trail occasionally throwing a stick in the bayou.

Ressie then asked Rev, "Rev, whens you gon stawd preachin da wud dat da creata wants ya to preach?"

"I'se always spoke da wud of da Lawd," Rev responded.

"Den whys is it when Massa Pederson drops yo surmons off at da churt fo you eva Sunday dat is whad use tells us an yo self too?" Ressie asked.

Rev appeared to try and recall a scripture to help him out with the question. He knew that he could tell Ressie how well the Lord had blessed him back home, but it would not be a relevant response. He turned back to see us waiting, like Ressie, for an answer. I shrugged my shoulders Aaron and Kat did the same. He seemed agitated. "I'se a shepawd fo da Lawd Miss Ressie and Massa knows dis. So would use radda haf me tells da wud or Massa Ugusta stands dere and tells ya?" said Rev, looking very satisfied with his answer.

Ressie, disappointed at Rev, said, "Fuss of all a wolf cain't tell a shepawd hows to watch da sheep and as fo whose gone teach da lesions maybe it don't madda. Its gone be da same lesson."

Rev, along with the rest of us, knew Ressie was right and his frustrations showed. He stopped and lashed out at Ressie. "I'se a man of God! I does whad I can to get da kind's like you to stop dat ol voodoo Afreecon stuff! Cuz da white man is in chawg! Yesdaday, today, ands tamarow! And it be time dat you an yo Afreecon God no dat." Rev was fuming his voice had reached the others. Ressie no doubt had struck a nerve with Rev. Apparently, Rev had been sensing that even during this time in history African people here in America view Christianity along with other

Western religions as void of real spirituality, and full, of dogmatic nonsense. That it had underlying motives to control and suppress one's true self, clearly not the original teaching of the one they call Jesus. We all stood watching, the gang, Lila, and Zeke. Rev looked at us all. He hadn't realized how vocal he had been. But, our being transformed, his confrontation with Aaron, fear of the unknown, and realizing Ressie sounded like some of his critics back home, became more than he could bear. Silence was felt throughout the bayou for a few seconds.

Just then the silence was broken. "Don't let huh puts no mojo on ya, Rev," Ward said.

"Shut up, Wawd!" Ressie yelled. She put both her hands on her hip, walked up in the face of Rev, and starred at him in a way that nearly scared him and us as well.

"Well! Well!" she said. "Use finely says whas on your mind-not whas on Massa's. Feels kinda goods don't it? Feels good to speak whas come out cha hawt not outta da book dat da man with a wup gaves ya. Tells me, Rev, hows come yo's and Massa's God is blessing only Massa? Huh? He writes down the surmon fo use to preach, and he gits da blessin and da fields, da hosses, da cotton, da corn and da big house. He gits him a woman and yo's woman too. Ya sees Rev my Ah-free-con God tells me ain't no man in chawg of a nudda man. My God tells me wees and Massa don't got da same God Rev, do ya know why? Cuz massa drank whisky and swinged from his porch while my sista's beaten and bloody body swung from an oak tree? Dat ain't da same God Rev? My Ah-free-con God tells me all of us aw da same. And dat any man whos thank udda dan dat ain't no man. Massa ain't no man of God and neder is you?"

Ressie's voice was trembling, but clear enough for Rev and the rest of us to hear. She ended by saying, "Not yestaday, not today, not tamara. If God done talks to ya likes ya say Rev, den use only doin wuk fo Rev?" She looked over at me and the others then back down the trail. "I'se ready ta finis my walk now."

Rev was completely shaken and embarrassed. He stood there in shame. There had never been a member, deacon, or fellow clergyman that spoke to him in such a manner. No seminary had prepared him and no scripture could bring him comfort at this moment. I signaled for the gang to go on ahead. Their heads hung low in shame for Rev. "Meet me in da clearing," I said.

I remained with Rev and put my hand on his shoulder as we began to walk back to the clearing.

"Ya alright?" I asked. Rev nodded, "Yes."

"It's always bedder da thangs like dat comes form people dat done been thru sumpin, ya know? Older peoples jus has dat affect I spose," I said.

We headed down to join the others as the sun began to set. We reached the big table in the clearing and found everyone sitting quietly, still feeling the after-shock from Ressie's testimony to Rev I had to give them an update on what I already had put together even if it wasn't a good time.

"Okay lisin up, Ya'lls needs to know whas happnin," I said, hoping my announcement would put life into their faces. Ward was the first to respond.

"I hopes dis news of yo's git us outta dis God fo saken hell," Ward said.

"Not just yet," I replied.

"Aw come on, John! Use spend haf da aftanoon down de unda dat tree wit dat ol voodoo woman."

I wanted to jump up and kick Ward's butt because I should not let him talk about Ressie that way, however I knew remaining calm was the best way.

"Sorry Ward but dere some thangs gots ta be done fuss," I said. "Whad I'm bout to tell ya'll may sound crazy but keeps in mind dat it cain't be no more crazy dan da fact dat wees here."

"Ya got dat right," Lizzy said.

"I'se fo one agree. Dere ain't nuddin you can say dat won't sound crazy dan us bein here," Aaron added.

"Specially if its gone git us home," Kat said.

"Gone on John, tell us whad cha known," said Rev.

I began to explain. "All dis goes back to da Buffalo Hill of 1999. Too many lies and wrong-doin been gon on in dis here town. As wees all know now, slavery did happen here, and if nobody believes dat den take a look around." I said this looking at Ward to let him know there was no denying that the Founder's day project was wrong.

"Wees all got blood ties and ancesta's from right here whey we stand. And de is puddy upset from da way wees all have been ackin."

Kerry said, "Ya know, I neva really paid attention to it, but my grandmama use to tell me aw roots go way back round by da bayo."

"Hey, John," said Lizzy. "I heard da same thang from my great-grandparents. Do ya believe da dey is round here on his plantation?"

"Hols on Lizzy," I said. "I'se got sumpin bedda dan dat. Back in 1999 when Bob Peterson gots all ya togedder he didn't have a clue whad he wuz doin." I looked at the faces on the gang. They were attentive, even Ward. I felt the strength that I had under the tree when Ressie told me I was to lead them.

I continued. "Bob thought ya'll wuz just celebrities and prominent peoples. He didn't know ya'all wuz some special peoples. Special cause ya'all ancesta's wuz burred in da cemetery da alls ya'll stawded to dig into. Ya'all wuz desacratin it and makin ya'll ancesta's mad."

"And das whys we here now?" asked Kat.

Ward added, "So Bob jus didn't pic anybody to heps wit his movie project. He pic six peoples who had kin folds burred dere?"

"Both of ya'all right," I answered.

"Man!" Aaron said. "Hows could we be so stupid? I neva did feels right bout doing dat whole thang."

"Me neder," Kerry said. "Lisnin to my dam agent again."

"Well John," Rev said, "Hows do we make things right wit dem?"

"I think I knows how but I'se ain't fo sho," I replied. "It goes back to da question Lizzy asked earlier bout aw ancesta's being here right now on dis plantation, and guess what? Wees dem."

"What?" Lizzy said.

The gang all started to mumble and grumble among each other as if everything else was easier to swallow. I motioned for them to calm down.

"Whada you mean, wees dem?" asked Ward.

"Look! Sadday at da surmonie, when dat black cloud came ova us, it had some kinda powa in it. When ya'll stuck dose shovels in da ground I blacked out," I said.

"Yeah! Das right," Kerry said.

Kat added, "I'se member not been able ta talk."

We began to swap our stories about the blackout and found we had all experienced the same feelings and sensations. I then reminded them how things were when we arrived.

"When wees showed up in dat cemetery it was noon time. And, according to Miss Ressie, dat's when wees all began to talk crazy," I said.

"So when we got here, aw 1999 minds jumped into aw 1831 bodies?" asked Rev.

"Fraid so, Rev," I replied.

"Is das why wees all got lives here?" Aaron asked.

Kat also added, "Das why does udder slaves ain't treatin us no diffrunt. Dey thank wees jus taking Mama Raylene det hawd."

Kerry asked, "So if we da ancestas at dis moment den jus like Rev said, hows do we make it right and go home?"

I explained, "maybe wees got ta make sumpin right wit awselves, Kerry. I'se don't know fo sho. But Ressie gaves me dis here information and I realized now dat aw ansah to get home is in three places."

"Cool!" Aaron said, "wheah dese places at?"

I replied, "One is in da cemetery, two is in aw minds, and three is inside da head of dat lady wees know as Ressie."

Ward asked, "Who is Mama Raylene? Whas aw relationship ta some of dese people? And whys eva body hates on me?"

I knew sooner or later someone would want to know all of this and I wasn't surprised that it was Ward, but I knew I had to side step his question.

"I'd love ta tells ya man, but its time ta turn in. Caleb da henchman is gon ride through here any second naw," I said.

Ward replied, "Yeah! Just whad I thought. He lets us know. Whad he wants us to," pointing to me and looking at the gang for support.

"Hey man!" I answered. "I'se told ya what I knows and I don't got time fo dis. Tamara is gon be rough. Wees all got ta wuk like wees been here all along. And if we don't got aw heads on right we might gits in big trouble. Tamara mawning, if it comes, will be like no other wees could eva thank of. So it bes be dat wees all turn in fo da night."

The gang still appeared bewildered by the information I shared with them. Somehow, they must have known it had to make sense and, if it didn't, all they had to do was take a look around. We all said goodnight and headed our separate ways. As I lay in what was my bed my mind was rambling with thoughts, scenarios and possible answers. I had hoped they would begin to realize the importance of committing or pledging to something like the theater without fully checking it out. Sometimes a prayer and a little trust in your people, especially our elders, can save you a lot of trouble. I prayed, asking God for strength, patience, wisdom, and a good-night's sleep. The sleep part was definitely not answered.

The sound of a cowbell rang as a horse trotted through the quarters. This had been the alarm clock for the hands of the Pederson Plantation for years. Faint lights from candles cast shadows from the clothes that were used as doors for houses and when the ringing ended every hand was up and dressed. Breakfast was bread, butter, cheese, and warm milk. If my history served me correctly, it would be the day's only food, from sun-up to sundown with water given to us occasionally. The only thing that would have any mercy on us would be the fact that it was the fall season. The days would be shorter and much cooler. As the morning sun slowly took its form in the sky, Kerry, Aaron, Lizzy and I joined the hands for the walk towards the field. Sleep had not come easy for us and it showed in our faces. We knew the inevitable had arrived. Ward, who was driving a wagon filled with big empty baskets, met us at the edge of the fields. The wagon also contained long and large crocker sacks. These were our only tools for a full day of labor. The gang and I paid close attention to the other hands while making sure we didn't end up first in line. The men picked up the sacks with a long strap attached and placed it over their heads and around their neck with the sack resting on their side. The baskets also had straps but they rested on the front of their body. As all the equipment for the day had been removed the hands stood huddled together quietly looking down the road that led to the mansion. Ward signaled the gang and me to the front of the wagon.

Ward said, "Dis mawmin a mean looking man woke me up and took me to da bawn to git dis supply wagon. Dis brudder had evil coming out his eyes, and wuz built like a linebacker. I didn't say a wud. Den he got a bell and told me to come here and waits fo um."

"Dat mus be Caleb," I answered. "Miss Ressie waned me about him and naw I'se gon waned ya'all. Dis ain't no ave-ege slave-hand. Ressie said he is deth on hossback so ya'lls be cool."

"I'se ain't gonna takes no mess from nobdy dis time of mawning," Aaron said.

Just then Ward said, "Speakin of da devil."

We turned and saw a man headed towards us on horse-back; the hands began to look nervous. Some tightened up their straps and others bowed their heads. Clearly all appeared agitated. We all watched the image that began to take the form of the man on the horse. As he slowed down the hands all came to an attentiveness that resembled a squad ready to receive their orders from their leader. He came to a stop, tugging at the reins of the horse that stepped side to side, back and forth. A clicking sound came through his teeth, signaling the horse to keep still once and for all, and it did, quickly obeying the rider's order. He sat there moving his head over us all surveying to see if everyone was present. The gang and I were in awe seeing why this henchman had the reputation that he did. He was a magnificent physical specimen, but mean looking. He seemed somewhat aged, but in good shape. His muscles ripped through the shirt that appeared to be too small. He was brown skin with a shaven head. His eyes were small and beady with crow's feet. I couldn't imagine where a man of his physique and features could have come from in this day and time. Aaron and Kerry tried not to seem intimidated, but the presence of this giant man was too much. I began to remember that this was the monster that beat and then hung my mother and God only knows how many other slaves. After surveying the hands to see if any were missing, Caleb spoke.

With a deep and commanding voice, he said, "Nah use niggahs lisen!" "Massa Bobby done told me dat da cone (corn) is ready to be hocked. Use wenches needs to take yo lil suckas (children) witcha ova to da fields. Nows tak ya'lls baskets and git, and no loafing. Da dey is shawt. If I'se haf ta I'll wup da black off ya back. As fo use udda niggas dat look like a man da same goes fo ya'll. Use bedder wuks extra hawd aw I'se gon tare off black skin all day long. Nah git cho coon asses on!"

We stood there stunned. Never before had I encountered or imagined a Black man like this. Aaron and Kerry began to look like the others, scared and totally defenseless against this mammoth of a man. Neither of us could have ever conjured up the hate and dislike to match what radiated out of the beady eyes and voice of Caleb. He was the perfect machine. A full-spirited Sambo, a black man who had been broken early on and taught to think and feel like his master. As the hands began to disassemble, I contemplated on the comparison of Caleb and today's Blacks. Along with being physically intimidating his self-hatred was immense. My research had taught me about the hatred of black skin worldwide. In Australia, the Prime Minister allowed the mix Aborigines to be adopted by the white citizens while the original dark-skinned population received a regret for colonization and remained poor. In Brazil, the mixed races are considered white. Even the dark-skinned Brazilian who achieves prominent economic status now classifies himself as white. Our Black celebrities have ridded themselves of their broad noses like Napoleon did to the Sphinx. Our women and mothers began early burning, pressing, and chemically inducing their hair to look like Europeans. They change their God-given natural hair to so-called good hair. Men took oaths and pledge loyalty to institutions and organizations they don't fully understand for political gain and prosperity at the hands of their people, while claiming brotherhood. They spend and pledge dollars on clothes and material possessions to maintain a status to respect while turning their backs on their children and communities. We let the unconscious, but well manifested, mindset of self-hatred continue to produce images. As a matter of fact we encourage it. Rather than let sitcoms of comedians and clowns diminish from prime time we fight for more. Presently, there is not a Black drama that reflects any seriousness, except the last seconds of a down-to-the-wire basketball game.

As I headed to the fields Caleb yelled at Ward, "Goes and takes da wagon to da bawn and prepare a team. Massa Claude is gon to get Massa Bobby from town."

We followed Zeke and the hands to the other end of the fields. They turned around facing the direction in which we came as though they would head back. Zeke pointed to the men to spread out. They all lined up in each row of cotton and began to pick. Aaron, Kerry, and I watched closely as they each went down their own row.

Kerry said in a low voice of astonishment, "Man jus look at um move."

"Yeah," I said, shaking my head with disgust. "Nudin but a programmed machined."

Aaron said, "Hey ya'll look at Zeke. Checks out hows he does it."

We began to pick according to Zeke. The left index and long finger pulled the cotton and the cloves it sat on from the stem. The tip of the thumb pried it back from the cloves and the right hand fingers were used to separate it from the cloves, throwing it in the sack. The cloves were prickly but we dared not express ourselves out loud. We started slowly, but we knew falling behind the others would only land us in trouble.

A few hours went by and it seemed we were now part of the well-oiled machine of cotton picking. I glanced up to see the progress that I had made in hopes that if I got through early I could lay off the rest of the day, obviously my twentieth century mind was playing tricks on me. The row I worked seemed endless and any idea I had of finishing early was erased. I looked up at the sun and figured it was about noon, wiped the sweat from by brow, and bore the stinging sensation of pain from the dirty sweat that entered the broken skin of my fingers. I checked around for Caleb who was behind me, far to the left. Aaron was on the next row to my left and Kerry to my right. I wanted to break the wall of silence to forget the pain that was coming from my back and fingers.

"Hey Kerry," I whispered, trying not to be heard by Caleb. "Dis here might be a lil hawda dan does two-a-day practices ya'lls have."

"Man two-a-days is a picnic compad to dis," responded Kerry.

"Yo Aaron," I called. "Dis here gon wuk all dat licar and dope outs yo system."

Aaron replied, "Dat may be, but when I'se get back I'm gon git drunk and smokes me one fo all da brudders dat wuk da fields."

Just then out of nowhere came a loud snap. Aaron screamed loudly as if he had been pierced with a knife. Kerry and I turned to see where Caleb had lashed his whip across Aaron's back.

"Wahd da hell is wrons wit use man?" Aaron yelled at Caleb.

Thinking quickly, I stepped over to Aaron and grabbed him. "No Aaron, No! Quiet man!" I said.

Caleb said, "Use bedder get a hol uh dat coon ass niggah fo I'se bead'em fo sho."

Kerry reached down and gave Aaron back his sack that had fallen. He was bleeding slightly, a long whelp across his back. His shirt was torn. Aaron starred at Caleb with retaliation. I begged him to stop and be cool.

I said calmly, "Just go on bac to wuk man let it go."

"Let it go my ass!" Aaron replied. "Dis niggah dissed me man!"

Caleb was stunned at Aaron's bravery and took it as a threat. He got off his horse and began to roll up his whip as if he were preparing to strike again.

"Dere sumpin use wanna say, Aaron? Hun!" Caleb added.

I desperately pleaded with Aaron again to let it go.

At that moment a wagon came up and Ward screamed, "Hey, Caleb! Caleb!"

Caleb turned back; it was Ward with Massa Claude. Caleb turned back to Aaron looking very angry then gave him a sly grin and said, "Use and I'se got bitness latah."

Aaron answered, "Whadeva."

My attention was now turned to the white man on the wagon, Claude Peterson. I looked at him starring as if looks could kill. Claude told Caleb to give his horse to Ward to take back to the barn and drive him into town.

Claude couldn't help but noticed the way I was looking at him. "Whad in tha hell use looking at me so crazy fo boy?"

The word "boy" that came from him although it made me angry I knew I could not retaliate since this was a matter I could not take personally. I had to set an example for Aaron. I looked humbly at Claude and said, "I'se not looking at 'cha no mo Massa Claude."

He shook his head at me. "Gone git cho Black asses back to wuk!" He yelled.

Let's go Caleb, I'm tired of looking at dese ol' niggahs."

They headed down the road that led off the plantation. As I watched them ride off, a desire to avenge the death of my mother and aunt came over me. I wondered how these two individuals, Claude and Caleb, could basically control nearly seventy human beings. Aaron and Kerry argued loudly as I watched the two monsters fade out of my sight.

I then heard a "Huh? Huh?" It was Aaron looking desperately for approval on the matter. "Whad?" I said.

"I said I'se ain't gon be able ta takes any mo of dis here mess," said Aaron.

I got in his face and said, "Next time, dere ain't gon be nobody ta stop him. And dat man will take all kinds of pleja in killin yo ass!"

Aaron just stood there. He knew that I was right, but couldn't help but feel that he must do something to Caleb who did not give him the respect he believed he deserved. We continued on with our work. The confrontation had put us behind the others. It was amazing that during all this commotion no slave had ever stopped working. They never flinched for a second. Apparently being well programmed made them immuned.

Although it was fall, the afternoon sun still made the men sweat. The only relief in sight was Kat coming our way with buckets of water being carried by a mule. She couldn't make it to us fast enough, as we met up with her to quench our dry throats. Kat couldn't help but notice the blood on Aaron's back.

She asked, "Whad in da wuld done happin to yo back Aaron?"

Kerry answered, "He caught da end of Caleb's whip."

Aaron then added, "It ain't nuddin, I'se can take it."

Kat said, "John, please don't let dis fool get killed!"

"I'se gon try Kat, but Aaron gon haf ta learn the hard way dat talkin crazy ain't good fo nobody."

But dat niggah dissed me! And I deserve respect. Kat replied, "respect is earned Aaron dis ain't da world of hip-hop and dat fake respect de tal'ks bout."

We finished our water break and returned to work. Kat made her rounds through the fields to Zeke and the others. Ward showed up again with a bigger wagon this time that seemed to be even deeper. Following the leads of the others we dumped whatever cotton we had picked into the wagon. Ward drove the wagon through and around the field every few hours throughout the day. As the sun began to set the sound of a clanging cowbell rang through the air. Zeke stood and motioned for us to head out of the fields. I had realized at this time that Zeke must have been like a lead man. He had waved us on to work and told us when to quit. We walked out between the rows of cotton. Ward was at the end of the fields holding the cowbell. We dragged our feet, but finally made it to the clearing. The field gang, Lizzy, Aaron, Kerry and I were worn out more than the regulars of course, and we did a bad job trying to hide it. Lila who had been work-ing in the cornfields with her kids was there to meet Kerry. Zeke stood patiently waiting for Lizzy to sit down to get a seat next to her. Kat and Rev came over from the mansion with food loaded on a wagon. Ressie was there waiting with a cloth that had been dipped in a mixture of ingredients. She had made a salve for Aaron. Kat had told her earlier what had happened and she made a trip over to the barn and down to the bayou and picked up a few things. She told Aaron to hold still as she placed the cloth over him. It didn't smell very well, but I could tell it felt great. I watched like a worried father.

Aaron asked, "Whas in da cloth Miss Rissie?"

Ressie, looking ever so calm said, "O…jus a lil fatback, some flowuz dat grow out da bayo wader, and some hoss droppins."

"Whad!" cried Aaron, as he unsuccessfully tried to knock the cloth away from Ressie. "Man is dis stuff gon make me bedder?"

"Wees gon see," said Ressie. "Unless use got a bedder medacine? But I done did dis many times befo and dose peoples all lived. So I reckon bes ya sat dere and shutup."

Aaron grimaced a little bit but did not say another word to his doctor. Ressie positioned the cloth on his back to where it would stay. The foul smelling aroma circled as we began to eat. Lila and Zeke did not seem to be bothered by it, so the gang and I ate with bittersweet feelings. We were more tired than hungry and the dinner menu of bread, grits, and warm milk did not increase what little appetite we had. We just knew we had to eat to maintain our strength. There was no time for socializing. Lila and Kerry said goodnight and headed for home; their three kids at their side. Slavery did not discriminate against age. If you could walk you could work.

Zeke turned to Lizzy. Having found the strength somewhere to smile, he asked, "Hows yo day gon?"

She look at him as if to say, "What the hell kind of question was that," rolled her eyes, but could not conjure up anything to say that could cut him down. "I lived. Hows yo day?"

Zeke replied enthusiastically. "Fine Lizzy, I'se git ta sits next ta ya and all. I'se cain't thank of a bedda way ta ends a day." She frowned at him and then turned away. He realized his advances of pleasantry were not working. The broad grin on his face now changed to a solemn expression. "I'se spose use real tired Lizzy." He stood up. "Use have a goodnight."

Lizzy was somehow clearly moved by the kindness and warmth of Zeke's personality. She checked us out as though she wanted our approval on something. Our expressions were solemn and heart-felt like Zeke's.

Kat said, "Girl, use knows dat man is sincere. I mean whad kinda game is he gon play on a plantation. You odda be nice fo once."

Lizzy knew Kat had a point. With all the work that had been put on us today this brother had no terms for her but to speak and see how her day went. She stood up to go after him. "Hey Zeke!" she yelled.

He turned back to answer, "Yea Lizzy?"

"Hows ja likes to walk me ta my cabin?"

The grin he had a minute ago reappeared. "Whys I would luv ta Lizzy."

As they headed to the women quarters the rest of us acknowledged how tired we were and decided to turn in. One of two little girls who was sitting next to Kat let out a big yawn and then tugged on her arm and said, "Mama? I'se seepy."

Rev and I glanced at each other quickly. Aaron awakened from his trance and said, "Mama? Whad is dese chilluns doin callin use Mama Kat?"

She hesitated to answer, seeming a little reluctant to explain the situation. She became teary-eyed and started to sniffle.

Ressie then stepped in and said, "Miss Ruth tolds me de bought dese two lil guls from a drifta bout a yea ago. Deys

Mama and Pappy wuz killed when day buned downs a nudda plantation. Dat drifta had bout five chilluns and a couple of men hands wit em. Massa Ugusta figas dose two lil guls wuz de only ones dat had no idea bout dat buning, so he boughts em."

Rev, Aaron, Kat and I starred at the two children. They sat innocently as we heard Ressie's story.

Kat said, "I'se knew dey was special. Massa Ugusta's wife, Ms. Ruth makes sho dey stay next to me to learn hows ta wuk in da big house."

She stood and picked up the little girl who was sleepy. Rev obliged picking up the other one. They both said good-night and headed to slave quarters of the big house each holding one of Kat's newly adopted kids.

Ressie removed the cloth from Aaron's back and said, "Das draws the so-ness outs of it. Use gon be fine in a nudda day or so."

I watched him stand slowly in pain. Hey man use gon be all right? Do ya need a hand ta make it to da house?" I asked.

"Naw man. Thanks, I can make it. I sho pre-shade whacha gave me Miss Ressie. Goodnight, ya'll."

Ressie and I both said goodnight. She then asked, "How yo day gon baby?"

I glanced around quickly making sure everyone had left the table. "Dis mawning when Caleb spoke to us and dens struck Aaron cross da back fo talkin, I realized dat whad cha says bout em is true. I also saw my Pappy Claude. I couldn't hep but looks at em with the thought of how he treated Paulene and Raylene."

Ressie replied, "Don cha make it stops yo's thanking on whacha godda do fo yo Moma and yo Aunt Raylene nah, ya here?"

"I'se here ya, Miss Ressie."

Just then a loud snap of a branch breaking came from the bushes across the clearing. Ressie and I stood up. "Yo who's dat?" I asked curiously. A figure then moved out running toward the big house, but it was dark and neither of us could make out whom it might have been, but I had a pretty good idea.

I asked Ressie, "Whey wuz Ward at dis evening?"

"He stood in fo Caleb early today wit da bell buts I'se ain't seen him since. He musta ate wit da house hands rader dan comes out heeh wit us. Does ya thank dat wuz Ward in da bushes?" Ressie asked.

"Who else at da big house would lisin in on us from da bushes. Caleb or da Pedersons don't have to run away," I said. I kissed Ressie on the forehead. "Goodnight, Ressie."

"Goodnight baby. Talks to da Lawd fo ya goes ta sleep naw, ya heeh?"

I made my way over to my house then pulled back the cloth door to see Aaron and Zeke pouring buckets of water in the washtub. Zeke tested the temperature with his hand.

"Feels alright Aaron. Bedder po one mo bucket doe. John's kinda long ya know."

Aaron asked, "All dis fo John?"

"Ya knows dis John's night ta go first and I'se goes afta him, answered Zeke, while wondering why Aaron did not know this. Aaron and I looked at each other and realized that much had not changed in 1999. Siblings still conduct this ritual of who bathes first.

Twelve hours of nearly non-stop labor, a worker getting disciplined, a long walk home, supper, minor conversation and a bath. I though if this weren't 1831 on a plantation, things would not be all that different for a lot of people back home. I finished my bath, laid down and reflected on the day. I watched Aaron sit in the small tub fighting back the pain as

Zeke poured water over his wound with a cup. I wondered if he would ever change his attitude about Caleb. I could not help but feel that at some point in time Caleb would retaliate for Aaron standing up to him. He obviously had found a friend in Zeke; the two seemed to be getting along pretty well. I assumed it was because Aaron was teaching Zeke to read. I prayed asking God for strength and understanding for my friends. I began to dose off as the cool night air blew through the holes of our house.

Chapter V

GOOD FRIDAY

Tuesday morning came very fast. Apparently, Caleb and Claude had returned during the late evening because Caleb was trotting through the quarters clanging the cowbell. The ritual that had taken place Monday morning began again right down to the same breakfast. The one thing that was different, however, was the fact that my lower back was stiff and my fingers were swollen. I walked out of the house with Zeke and Aaron who seemed to move a little better despite his wounds. The rest of the field gang appeared as I did. Kerry and Lizzy were walking with a slight limp, their eyes swollen from the lack of sleep, hard labor, and the hard beds.

We reached the edge of the fields and got our sacks and baskets for the day. Caleb was waiting at the entrance to the fields and already had summoned the house hands to come out this morning. The older hands, kids, and the barn hands were also present. I saw Rev and Ward sitting anxiously on the supply wagon. Rev gave me a look with his eyes that hinted something was up. Ward didn't make any eye contact with me, which confirmed my belief that it was him who was prying around the cabins trying to listen to the conversation that Ressie and I had last night. Caleb then announced that Master Bobby was back from town and had something to tell us before we started work. Caleb turned toward the mansion as two men on horseback headed our way. The hands waited patiently and quietly for the two men to approach. As they got closer I could tell one of them was Claude. The other one I couldn't see clearly. I knew it had to be Bobby the other brother. His face became clear as the morning sun gave way shining on the black hat that he wore.

"Oh my God," I whispered with shock. Kerry, Aaron, Kat, Lizzy, and I quickly glanced at each other, as if for an explanation. I looked at Rev and Ward on the wagon and they too had the same expression of disbelief. The man in the black hat, Master Bobby, was none other than Bob Peterson of Peterson Industries, or his ancestral twin. I quickly motioned to Kat and the field gang by putting my finger on my lips to keep quiet. I signaled to Rev to do the same but it was too late for me to warn Ward.

He screamed, "Oh my God, it's Bob!" The sight of seeing the person who appeared to be his boss back home caused an emotional rush and temporary memory loss as to where he was. Ward jumped off the supply wagon and ran to Bob as if he were a young boy running to meet his dad after a hard day's work. The gang and I were stunned. It was too late for me to do anything.

Rev yelled, "Ward! Ward!" but he ignored Rev's cry.

Ward ran up to Bob's horse screaming, "Bob! Bob! Wee's sho glad to see ya! We needs yo hep on dis nightmare das happnin. Dat ol fool John is behind all dis! I knows naw maybe use can hep us go home." Ward then turned to where I was standing eyeing me like the kid who ratted out his big brother to their father for playing with his power tools while at work. Bob didn't say a word; he just looked at Ward.

"Shut up and git back on dat damn wagon boy!" said an angry Claude. "I thought you were the one who had half a brain round here."

Bob then said, "Wait a minute. If there is something going on here I think that we should know. Don't cha agree Claude?"

Claude answered, "Yeah I guess but after you give them the news they might have a change of mind."

"Maybe so big brother, now you get back on the wagon and shut up. I'll talk to you later," said Bob to a surprised but dejected Ward.

Bob turned to us. "Under my daddy's request and with the money my family has worked so hard for, I went to Galveston and did some business. Now the kind of business that I had to do was because of what went on here at Peterson Plantation with that Raylene woman and her African magic. My daddy said it would be in our best interest that some of you niggers be sent off and we bring in new ones with fresh minds. So this upcoming Friday we will do just that. I bought some new hands and I'se also sold some of ya'll off. As far as who that is, well, let's just say this ain't going to be no Good Friday. He and Claude both laugh heartily as Caleb gave a deep and wicked grin. They told us to have good day, jerked back the reins on their horses still laughing off the announcement that resonated with so much fear.

They rode off back to the mansion as Caleb yelled to the scared looking hands. "Don't jus stands dere likes dumb mules. Git dose baskets and hit da fields. Some of ya'lls days aw numbad. I'se don't wants ta haf ta ends it soona."

For the first time the hands showed some expression on their faces. The spirit that had kept them alive and functioning in this oppressive time had left momentarily with the news of loved ones being sent off. Sold from one plantation to another is the worst nightmare of slave life. In exactly three days families and friends would be torn apart. Kids might be separated from their parents along with wives and husbands never to be seen or heard of again. People who cherished family as the soul reason of duty to love and to live in there times will be ripped apart in a whim. Lila starred at Kerry helplessly as he tried again to reassure her that she and the kids would stay together, but he was not doing a very good job. Zeke eyed Lizzy as though the next three days would tear up any idea he had of them having a life together. The innocent boyish grin he usually had in her presence had been erased. Aaron and Kat both looked at each other and realized this may be more than just a rap duo going their separate ways. She also held the two little girls by her side wondering about their fate and who would take care of them. Rev and I checked out the hands. We knew they had seen this before. They turned and went off to the row of fields while not giving much talk to the news. Their faces said a lot. Most of them knew this was more painful than any beating any one of them could ever receive. A person can heal from a beating but to see a family member sold off no one ever heals completely.

I shifted my attention to Ward who was sitting sheepishly on the wagon wondering why Bob spoke to him like that. Ward will now try anything to get in Bob's good graces, even doing something that may stop us from returning home. He thinks it might get him some brownie points just like the things he does so often back at Peterson Industries.

The gang and I walked off to our rightful places in the field. I looked around to see if Caleb was in sight. I didn't see him. Kerry working in the next row had the same idea.

"Hey John", he said. "Whos ya thank gon be sent off?"

I answered, "Don't know Kerry. Nobody does sept da massas."

"I'se hope dat Lila and da chilluns stays two geddar ya know," Kerry said with worry in his voice.

Aaron added, "I'se knows how ya mus feel Kerry but use gon haf ta hold on if they does. Use godda thank bout yo self stayin so wees all can get bac."

I heard Aaron's comment to Kerry. I knew that Aaron meant well and was right, but I saw that for maybe the first time, Kerry was thinking of someone other than himself. This was an attitude he wasn't known for back home. Although he talked team first in front of the cameras and in the newspapers. His play off the court was none other than for selfish reasons. I stayed quiet for the rest of the day as Ward made his rounds through the fields. I worked hurriedly trying not to think about us having to stay as long as Friday and possibly being sent off, but the thoughts of the announcement worried me terribly.

As the workday came to an end silence swept over the slave quarters. After supper the hands retired for the evening I stayed behind and sat on top of the big table in the clearing. I watched Zeke and Lizzy in front of one of the cabins that housed the women. They were embraced in a kiss. Their shadows were cast on the ground under the full moon. I smiled, but not for long. I gazed at the stars in the clear night sky thinking about the seasons. The fall had always been my favorite season and I felt how it was the most romantic time of year. I again watched Zeke and Lizzy knowing that Zeke may be sent off. This brother was very obedient and a hard worker who could easily fetch a hefty price on the auction block. It might also break Lizzy's heart because she had finally met someone who genuinely admired her unconditionally. The sound of a horse was heard in the distance. It was Caleb making his nightly rounds. I got up quickly and ran to my house. I reached for the cloth door at the same time as Zeke. He blew out the candle that Aaron had lit as the sound of Caleb's horse faded away.

Zeke quietly said, "I'se in luv John! I'se in luv with Lizzy."

I was really at a lost for words. Aaron was sleep and couldn't bail me out. There was no sincere answer I could give Zeke so I replied, "Das wunderful Zeke. I'se thank Lizzy's a good woman."

As he gave a little laugh I felt his innocent boyish love for Lizzy, but I also felt the sadness he may experience on Friday. It was amazing how Zeke had shifted his focus and energy into Lizzy despite the announcement today. I guess it's something one would need to do in order to keep from worrying and thinking about it. It had become a tool for protecting one's sanity, but only on the outside. I said my prayers and covered up with a wool blanket that felt like Velcro. I wanted to break the chill of the night air. The sounds of crickets made their way into the cabin. I lay on my back thinking of the events of the day and how some of the gang might be sent away. I couldn't believe that only a few days ago I really did not care about them and now here I am laying here like a worried father wondering how not only to take care, but save his family, as well. A night owl perched in a nearby tree supplied the music that put me into deep thought and eventually a deep sleep.

Wednesday morning seemed to come fast as Caleb's bell rang through the quarters. I didn't even remember hearing the rooster crow. The nightmare of the upcoming dreaded Friday was in my head. I'm sure every hand on the plantation was feeling the same anxiety. I did manage to tolerate the aches and pains a little better because I knew they would be present this time. The mood at the breakfast table was somber and not a word was spoken. Afterwards we made it to the supply wagon and I noticed Ward wasn't on it. Rev with Caleb watching us closely managed to give me an eye that there was something up. Maybe an explanation for Ward's absence would be shared. Later that afternoon on a water break he told me to have the gang remain at the clearing after supper.

The work today was hard as usual. I could see where we were making some kind of progress in the fields if that meant anything. I stayed silent while attending to the rows. There were so many things on my mind about what the future held for us should we never find a way home. And if we all came together, do we lose our chance should anyone of us get sold off and disrupt the energy? How could we then try to escape, or do we just endure here forever? The day finally ended as we completed nearly half the fields. There were conversations going on with the hands throughout the quarters. Rumors began to mount about mothers, fathers, children, and relatives who may be sent off. Boy was this like all other jobs when the news of layoffs would circulate throughout the plants, offices and warehouses in our day and time. But there was always a family to go to for support and another job to go and find. As the conversations ended and the regular hands retired the gang, Ressie and I, minus Ward became attentive to an anxious Rev.

Rev began "Las nite fo's I turned in I went ta go find Ward who wuzn't in his bed. I heard voices in da kichen sounding jus like Ward and Massa Bobby. Sos I tipped closa down da hallway wheys so I could hear bedder an I does. Ward wuz beggin and pleadin to do anythang not ta be sent off. Bobby asked Ward why should he keep him here. Ward told him dat he would let him know evathang that was gon on in da qwadas. Bobby den told Ward he may be able to do sumpin fo him if he could tells him sumpin dats wuthwhile." When Ward said, "Yes sur Mr. Pederson." Then Mr. Pederson looked at Ward real strange. I thought Ward wuz in trouble fo saying Mr. but Master Bobby grins at Ward and tells him don't call him "Mr." no mo not until we gets back home ta 1999."

"Wahd!" I yelled. "Rev aw you sho?"

The gang was all mystified. "How could dis be?" asked Lizzy.

"Man hol up ya mean dat Bobby really is Bob Peterson?" inquired Kerry.

Kat and Aaron were equally puzzled and sat there surprised at Rev's story. Ressie said nothing.

"But dat ain't all," said Rev. "Bob told Ward he had ta see if he could trust'um das why he didn't let on and dat Ward wuz diffrunt dan da res of us. He also told Ward dat da board of directas was probly wukin right now on a way to get us back home. Bob den promoted Ward to his assistunt right dere in da kichen and says dat spot is open back home too. Den came da real scary pawt. Bob said to Ward trust only him and he would make sho dat da Voodoo woman Ressie and John disappear and he would leaves um here to die. Dat John will no longer bees a problem to da good folks in Buffalo Hill. Tolds him he sees to it personally."

Ressie grabbed my hand squeezing it tightly she raised it up and kissed it.

Rev continued, "Ward tells Bob use is wuking on a plan ta do sumpin and dat Ressie gave hep. Den Bob told Ward he wanted him to drive him to Galveston dis mawning and esplanes how's we crossed ova and hows we plan on gon home. "Den I heard Massa Claude comin and I lef."

"If hees so confident dat da boad of directas is wukin to git us back, dew whys duz he wants ta know howz we crossed ova," said and angry Lizzy. "Cuz his dumb ass don't know, hees jus waitin like da rest of us," added Aaron

We were struck by Rev's information. We were, however, surprised at Bob or Bobby as he was in this day. I glanced at

Ressie for strength while the gang mumbled softly about what they'd just heard.

I asked confidently, "Is dere anyone at da table who feels da same as Ward bout all dis?" I gave them time to speak but no one said anything.

"I'se agree with Lizzy, I'se git da feelin dat Bob is usin Ward and givin him false hopes bout eva thang. Da reason being is dat if Bob wuz confident that the board of directa's wuz wuking to get us home why would he need to know hows we crossed ova?" said Rev.

"Dat damn sell out house niggah," said Aaron.

Kat added "I'se neva met a brudder like dat be fo in my life."

Lizzy and Kerry both asked, "Whad do we do?"

I said, "Fuss wees mus not lets Ward knows wees on ta him and Bob. Naw I'se need fo ya'll ta promise me dat ya stay strong and smawd cuz ya gon be tempted to sell out to da res of us." They responded in agreement. I held Ressie's hand through all of this.

"I'se gon make ya'll a promise. Dat I'se gon find us da way back and dat I won't let ya'll down. Jus trust each udder, pray and we gon make it."

Zeke and Lila headed towards us. Lizzy and Kerry knew this was their cue to leave. They said good night and went to their homes. The rest of us sat there pondering Rev's story.

Rev said, "Ya know John dat really done sumpin ta me ta hear dat boy talk like dat bout chu and Ressie. I member at college how not one time did I learn anything that wuz really spirichal. Dat somebody likes you and Ressie shows me dat anyone who gives sincere reverence to God, and produces luv and respect of his fellow man then dat is all God has eva acks of any man. Standin fo him use stands fo sumpin and when you don't, use rely on yo own wisdom and falls fo anythang. I done heard dese wuds from Malcolm and Martin dese two diffrunt men on one hand but da same on da udder. Deys bof got killed and maybe das why lot's uf preachas scayed to teach da trut. Dis is da fuss time I feel likes I could truly die fo whad God done led me ta beleve in and know its not always whad da doctrene said. Dis day and time fo any African to member his self is ta have his self-respect even if hees uh slave." Rev turned to Ressie and me with Aaron and Kat listening.

"Use right Miss Ressie. Use right ah-long. Hadn't been wuking fo God; been wuking for Massa and myself: specially in 1999."

"Das all right Rev, Das all right," answered Ressie.

Rev said goodnight to us and left for the big house. What he said was touching. There wasn't a TV or a big audience to support him, nor an offering given to support his cause. The man who had baptized some of the gang and me had finally heard the real message to his calling. There is only one God that lives inside each of us and as long as people live under that truth then death is not feared.

Kat and Aaron stood up. She gave him a hug. "Dis time las week we wuz throwin down wit some def lyrics at da club like dere wuz no tamara."

"Yea dat wuz wild," replied Aaron.

"Ya know John," said Kat. "It would be hawd to remain a slave here. I's miss my two guls back home. I do beleve use gon git us home den I'm gon worry bout da two guls I'se gon leave here. But I'm gon make sho I ain't gon be no slave in 1999. Goodnight cha'll."

The three of us stood there watching as Kat headed to the big house. Aaron's attention then turned to the couples in front of the houses. Kerry and Lila stood in front of their house and embraced. Zeke and Lizzy were also standing in front of the women's home holding hands and talking quietly.

Aaron shook his head. "Man dose boys noses is wide open. Minds me of my lil brudda back home can't tells en nuddin. Guess I'se gon have to break up da pardy's. Besides I'se godda teach Zeke haws ta count tonight. Night ya'll." Aaron said as he went to go spoil our roommate Zeke's date.

Ressie starred at me. Seeing the concern on my face she asked, "Ya know da bes thang is ta not tells dem da whole trut bout dey selves."

"Wishes I could doe Ressie. Maybe I can if I thank its da right time." I said sadly.

She replied, "Naws das de sign of a ledah."

I leaned down and kissed her rough cheek. "Goodnight Miss Ressie."

As I started for home the sound of a horse was heard in the distance. I made it in and lay on my bed as Aaron blew out the candle. I listened to the bits of wood popping in the potbelly stove, and thought back on the day remembering my friends and Ward. I began to realize that the first part of us getting back home really did exist with us finding out about ourselves. It was as if we were all learning a very valuable lesson about unity, though we were all different, we were all the same. A couple of nights ago I lay here defining the gang as Sambos. Now again I can't sleep for worrying about them in some way or another.

We all seemed to be different, yet we all seemed the same. Egos, emotions, fears and anxiety seemed to have gotten us where we are right now. To add to all that, none of us had truly gotten to know who we really were as individuals. Even I and my, "It's all Black or nothing at all" mind set. I realized in some way I had blocked myself from knowing so much more. I contemplated on all of this and the changes I would make should we all make it back, remain here or try to escape; anyway it wouldn't be easy.

The night passed through quickly. The cowbell rang on this Thursday morning no different than the other. I got up thinking would there be any announcements of threats made by the masters or Caleb. We met up at the edge of the fields as usual. Caleb was there on horseback. Rev was driving the supply wagon while Ward was in Galveston with Bobby. My primary concern was how much information he would give to Bob. Caleb held us in check while looking back toward the big house. I could feel something going down. All the hands were there just like the morning they announced that some of us were leaving. I looked over at Rev to see if he knew anything. He shrugged. Apparently, he didn't know anything about an announcement. The slaves were about to walk to the fields when Claude came riding back from the mansion. He came to a stop and got right down to business... with a stern look his eyes moved back and forth thru the crowd of slaves.

"It has been brought to our attention that somebody has been reading!" He quickly eyed Zeke. Zeke's facial response was a dead giveaway. He was shocked and afraid that he had been found out. The fear quickly spread through the crowd like a gasoline laden trail that had been lit. Claude knew now that the information he had been given was correct.

"I want all mothers and children up front near the wagon," yelled Claude.

The gang and I nervously watched as the female hands and children made their way up front. You could hear crying and whimpering start to make its way through the crowd. Claude signaled for Caleb to get down off his horse and pull out the slave who dared to try and educate himself. Caleb walked toward the men slaves and stood in front. Lila began to shake. Kerry nodded his head to her. He was okay. Caleb then made his walk through the men and stopped in front of Aaron towering over him. Aaron stood his ground. I thought this was it. Aaron had been teaching Zeke to read and maybe they found the book in the house. Caleb had promised Aaron he would pay him back. Could I let Aaron get whipped or killed? Do I need to jump in and get shot myself, never giving the others a chance to get home? They both just starred at each other like two prizefighters before the big match.

Just then Claude screamed, "God damn it Caleb! Get to it! That nigra's been making a fool outta my family!" Caleb reached at Aaron but extended his hand behind him and grabbed Zeke.

"Tie him to the wagon," Claude yelled at Caleb and told Rev "Keep the wagon still!"

The hands stood motionless. I grabbed Aaron so he wouldn't try anything stupid. But we all knew that the whipping would happen because Ward had sold out before he left for Galveston. Caleb pulled Zeke over to the wagon as Claude cocked his gun. He tied Zeke's left wrist to the wagon rail and then tied his right wrist to the other end. His arms were about two feet apart as his back faced the crowd. Caleb went over to this horse to get his whip.

Claude again addressed the hands. "I'm doing the rest of ya'll a favor by teaching this boy a lesson. If he learns to read then he might educate himself, run away and make things harder on ya'll. Remember the less ya'll know and think about the better off ya are. My family will always provide fo yo welfare. That means yo food, clothing, and a place to stay. That's our agreement with ya'll."

I listened angrily and helplessly realizing all the things I had studied about plantation overseers making men into slaves, but spiritual or physical slavery could never come close to what I was about to see. The words that came out of Claude's mouth and the whipping Zeke was about to receive was too much for a people. Africans had already been separated from their families, culture, spirituality, language, and their own way of life. This slowly conditions their minds even more. Over 70 men, women, and children stood at attention with the gang and me. And here are these two men one white with a gun and believing the Lord on his side, the other a model of sheer force. He was a physical specimen who had already been mentally conditioned to the highest form of self-hatred. I had seen so many black people destroy each other, some at the hands of drug dealers, who I considered to be the biggest Sambos. Others through gang violence, fighting and defending a territory own by the powers that be. Drive-by's, and other crimes against one another, backbiting, gossiping, spreading rumors around their jobs, neighborhoods, churches and even their own homes, but never anything in such a public forum. Claude began a stare down with me. It was obvious Ward had told him I was the leader; the man making all the plans. His own belief that staring at me while Zeke's beating took place would somehow strike fear into my mind. A part of me felt that I should show some fear to keep the situation as it should be in this day, but I could not because of the ancestors' spiritual strength running warm through my veins. Since we both knew who the other was there was no love lost. He raised his arm up in the air never taking his eyes off me. There was no doubt now Ward had told Bob and Claude of my plans. Yes sir, Ward B. Shaw, a five hundred-dollar, suit-wearing specimen of pure trained butt kisser. Corporate America's answer to the new and improved Sambo, I starred back at Claude swearing to my self that I would not flinch or take my eyes off him during this ordeal. I refused to watch. He continued to hold his arm in the air hoping that the anxiety would be just as deadly to the hands.

There was silence with only the whimpers of women and children. Claude spit on the ground while never losing eye contact with me. He slowly lowered his hand. Caleb reared back with the force of a javelin thrower and snapped the whip. The sound that followed was blood curdling. No one in the gang had ever heard such a scream. The sound of the women crying was gut wrenching. Again, Caleb displayed his marksmanship. His years of punishing Africans had made him void of spirit. Zeke tried hard to fight back the pain while turning his head to find Lizzy in the crowd for strength. She was there standing and watching with sheer horror etched on her face. She made eye contact hoping he would stay strong. They both failed, as Caleb continued to strike Zeke across his back the gang watched. The flesh on his back started to open. One more strike and his knees buckled. The way Caleb had tied him to the wagon hindered his knees from touching the ground. Zeke just hung by his wrist. As Caleb struck again and again, the sound that came from Zeke was no longer a scream. It did not even sound like that of a human, but it was a helpless plea for mercy.

Claude then yelled, "Up!"

Caleb stopped in motion like someone had pulled the cord on a machine. Claude broke his stare with me and surveyed the faces of the slaves. They were catatonic, not moving and not crying anymore - just looking at Zeke hanging there.

Claude told the slaves, "Let this be a lesson to all of ya'll who goes against my family." You are here on this land and in this great country to work for my person that is an agreement that goes back to that God forsaken dark place called Africa. You niggers just can't seem to see how better off y'all is. We feed you, clothe you, we teach about the real God out

125

of our bible, we even lower ourselves sometimes and have children with ya. Now why can't you just work like good niggers and leave trying to read; believing in that African religion and running off alone. He waved for Caleb to cut him down. Zeke fell to the ground his wounds absorbed the soil.

Caleb got on his horse. "Ressie! Takes care of Zeke," he turned to the other hands. "Git cho Black buhinds ta wuk."

Ressie summoned Lizzy to help her with Zeke. Kerry and I picked Zeke up and put him in the wagon. "Ressie gon take care of ya Zeke." Sadly I said, "Use gon be al rite. Just hang in der."

Zeke lay there with the life nearly out of him. He mumbled a few words but no one could seem to understand them. A tearful Aaron leaned into the wagon with his voice trembling. His tough gangster image was shattered. He was simply Aaron, a young man who had just witnessed his friend nearly beaten to death and for no reason other than because he was an African. An African man, a slave forced to accept the fact that he could not read, write, count, or learn anything for fear that he might educate himself and learn the truth of his condition and leave his master.

Aaron looked at Zeke. "I'se sorry man. I'se so sorry Zeke. I'se didn't means to git ya's in trouble," Aaron said mercifully. I put both my hands on his shoulder, holding him back as Rev began to pull off Zeke tried to talk.

"Keeps quiet Zeke," Lizzy said.

Aaron quickly went back to the wagon.

"Aaron…. Aaron," Zeke said clearly having barely enough strength to talk.

"Yeah Zeke, I'se right here," Aaron answered.

Zeke said, "Nots yo…. nots yo fault Aaron. I'se done anythang ta be da man dat Lizzy needs." He began to cough repeatedly. He opened his eyes to see Lizzy in the wagon, "I'se.... lub.... ya...Lizzy."

Lizzy covered her mouth. She was completely over-whelmed by what she had just heard. No longer able to hold back she began to cry passionately. Never before had a man risked his life and limb to be somebody who she had con-vinced herself she needed. The men whom she intimidated, the ones she laughed at who tried to buy their way into her life, the ones who were just never able to match her stan-dards, her dreams, and her goals would never be the man that Zeke revealed himself to be. She stood beside the wagon and held Zeke's trembling hand. His tears fell quietly as the wagon headed back towards the quarters the gang headed to the fields. Still expected to do no less work than any other day the psychological effect to act as if nothing has happened was what I felt. I again looked at how this energy is still run-ning in 1999. Black folks being immune to so many injustices that we not only stop fighting a community fight - that shows in our neighborhood – we have stopped fighting to raise our kids in a respectable manner. The pressure and pain to fight back has made us give up on so many things, most damag-ing of course is our minds, and some of us have completely lost them. Operating only on what society, politicians, teach-ers, church leaders and everything outside of ourselves to dictates how we should live. Completely ignoring the true God and the divine energy within us. That spiritual energy that tells us every minute that we are alive and blessed, and to trust what we feel instead we throw away this light and head towards the darkness of a conditioning that has taught us to trust only man.

The morning had come to pass. Ressie and Lizzy worked on Zeke. Rev and Kat returned to the house to prepare lunch for the Petersons. As the workday ended silence and heartache was again the mood at the clearing. After a sunset supper the gang remained seated for updated information. Ressie announced that she and Lizzy had patched up Zeke with the medicine cloth, and that he was resting and would be okay.

Aaron, who was understandably taking this hard, knew Ward was the real blame here but couldn't get to him because Ward was gone. Still he had to vent some frustration.

"Man when I sees dat Ward I'm gon kick his sellout wanna be like Caleb Black behind."

"Den dat will make two field hands Caleb gits da beats on." I replied.

"I'se knows whey Aarons coming from," added Kerry. "Wees wuking aw fangers till wees see da blood drop out. Wuking hawd like twenty fo seven. I'se figad Ward wuz pawt of da seven of us."

"Lawd! Wees need yo help," cried Rev.

Kathy was looking somberly at Lizzy who wasn't eating. The whole gang appeared to be coming apart, while Lizzy was not eating and her head was hanging down. Kat began to cry. Aaron and Kerry were both talking at the same time about what to do to Ward when he got back. And Rev was having a one-man gospel explosion praying and calling on God for help. I suddenly noticed something very strange while trying to raise my voice over theirs without being too loud. Ressie was holding one hand over her mouth the other hand was held up high in the air as tears streamed down her face.

"Hol up! Hol up!" I yelled. "It's Ressie! It's Ressie! They all quickly settled down. Lizzy even raised her head to see what was going on with Ressie. I moved over to where she was sitting and sat down next to her.

A sniffling Kat asked, "Whas wrong Miss Ressie?"

I was concerned with Ressie, I put my arms around her and said, "Miss Ressie talks ta me! Whas wrong?"

She let down her hand and removed the other from her mouth. Through the trembling voice she said, "I'se member....I'se member..I'se member it all now," pointing to Kerry as she said this. We were all confused. "K-ree..K-ree, says it."

I knew Ressie wasn't crazy, but she wasn't making much sense either. "Calms down Miss Ressie," I said.

She said, "I'se heard K-ree say it." "Said whad?" I asked.

She replied, "Whad Raylene tells me bout da seven."

I stood quickly turning to Kerry. "Hey man whad you say bout da numba seven?" I asked emphatically. Kerry quickly tried to remember what he had said earlier.

"Uh...uh," studdered Kerry.

"Okay, Okay man. Jus take it easy and trys ta member," I said begging.

Kerry calmed down. "Uh.... I said dat wese spillin aw blood and we wuking twendyfo-seven and Ward is pawt of da seven dat came here."

"Das it. I'se member naw John," said Ressie.

"Members whad John? Whas she talkin bout," asked Rev. "Yea man whas up," Aaron added.

"Fo Moma Raylene died she told Ressie uh story dat we wuz coming and in dat story it says howz da numba seven brang us here and hows it takes us home" I explained.

"Whys use ain't tell us dis befo Miss Ressie?" Lizzy asked.

I answered for Ressie. "She couldn't member cuz of Moma Raylene's det."

As she began to calm down, Ressie said, "Yea, evathang is all cleah naw. I'se can tell ya'll whad Raylene said. Ya'll come closa. John use gives me yo hand."

I gave Ressie my hand. She closed her eyes and began to slowly rock back and forth. She began to hum a little.

"Deys coming," Ressie said.

"Whos coming?" asked Rev.

"Da ancestas," I said. "Now be quiet."

The gang seemed to be intrigued and a little scared but not totally convinced. Then a soft wind blew through the clearing. An owl echoed loudly and clearly as to signal the arriving of something. The gang was now completely spooked. Their faces were attentive to Ressie whose eyes were closed with a peaceful smile.

"Yo Aunt Raylene is here John."

I hesitated but I knew I had to show my belief in her. I spoke up, "Hi Aunt Raylene. Hows are ya?" The gang was petrified as I turned to see their faces.

Ressie continued. "Raylene says use got yo Momma's eyes." She then hesitated. We looked in silence with our faces numb. She continued, "Raylene says is all like da cree-ata's wuk." In seven days, seven peoples will come in da twelf awa of da high sun and dese seven will come to know da ancestas. And at de end of seven days and seven nights da blood of an unbroken African man mixed wit da blood of a untouched African woman mus be put on da heads of dose seven at da place of de ancestas at de time of da fuss hi sun." She let go of my hand, opened her eyes, and let out a deep breath. The calm breeze came to an end.

The silence of the gang gave the indication they were spooked or that they believed Ressie was crazy, but they surprised me.

Aaron was the first to speak. "Naw I hear ya naw esplanes it to me."

Kerry added, "Yea man hows dis seven stuff spose ta gits us home."

I began to explain to them what I heard from Ressie as best I could. "Bares wit me now. Wee's arrived here Sadday noon dat we done all agreed on. Seven days from dat is Friday."

"Ya means wees can go tamara at noon?" asked Aaron.

"No you dummy Miss Ressie said at da end of seven days and seven nites," answered Kat.

Rev added, "And da fuss high sun is noon das aw cycle ya'll! Noon Sadday ta noon Sadday."

I was proud of the gang's involvement. Their trust and confidence in Ressie and me meant a lot in all this madness. Lizzy appeared a little sceptical though. She got down on her kness and grasped a stick.

"I'se gon to see fo sho," she said, looking up at us and pointing the stick at me. "Nah let's see." She began to scribble in the dirt for about a minute while the gang and I looked at her and each other. Ressie continued to hum during all this. Lizzy then quickly stood up, dropped the stick, and covered her mouth. Something seemed to scare her.

"Oh-my-God," she whispered.

I put my hand on her shoulder and asked, "Lizzy whad is it? Whas going on?"

She answered, "Ressie's right. I added it up. Each day is twendy-fo owa's seven days times twendy-fo awa's is 168. When I took dat 168 and subtracted it from 1999 it comes out ta be 1831."

"I'se guess dis ain't no voodoo cuz numba's don't lie," responded Rev. He was now a true believer in Raylene's prophecy.

"Amen Rev," I said. "Now wees knows dat wees gon ta stay here ta Sadday. But dere is still some questions gon ta be ansad. One is geddin evabody to da cematery fa noon on Sadday."

"And da second is geddin Ward ta go along wit dis cuz Miss Ressie said dat da seven of us gots ta go togedder," said Kerry.

Rev added, "Whas dis bouts blood from people and pudding it on aw heads? I'se not fo sho dat's sits well wit me."

Lizzy responded to Rev, "It's gon sit well wit ya if its gon git all of us home."

"Das right Lizzy," Kat added. "Dis jus ain't bout you Rev."

Rev said, "Ya'll right. But wad is an unbroken man and untouched woman?"

I explained, "An unbroken African man is somebody dat has not been convurded to da white folks ways. He still has his African mind. An untouched African woman has not slept wit a white man. Man whey da hell wees gon fine somebody by wit dose credenchalls round heeh?" Aaron asked in frustration.

"Hey John. I wuz curious just who wuz Moma Raylene? Whas huh connection to you and evabody here?" asked Lizzy.

I wanted to answer Lizzy's question, yet I still didn't think it was a good idea since they knew their kinship to Ward. I hesitated to give an answer. The sound of a horse could be heard in the distance. It was Caleb making his nightly quarter check and saving me from an explanation. I helped Ressie up as the others took off not having time to say goodnight.

Ressie said, "Run on baby! Caleb sees me all hees gon do is watch me walk home, but he will tah yo hide."

I kissed her quickly and ran to my house. My thoughts were bittersweet. I was happy that we found how to get back home but getting all the ingredients together was a major problem. The idea that one of us may be sent off was the immediate problem since that would be found out tomorrow. I just lay there again contemplating how to deal with that possibility. Thinking how the numbers all added up and the transformation getting here this could only be the work of

African spirituality or the Ifa system. Ifa means universal knowledge however it deals a lot with sciences they consider sacred; geometry, physics, astrology, astronomy, etc. many systems throughout the diasporas came from Ifa which itself was born in the Nile Valley. It also teaches how our subconscious stays at war with our conscious. The subconscious operating on the conditioning factor tricks our conscious. I have understood through studying that these sciences help the conscious with internal conflict. Our ancestors and priests know this and taught this to the people at times. But since we had this knowledge taken away from us I see now how important it is to get it back. Universal knowledge teaches us spiritual transformation even here in 1999. I fell asleep for a brief moment as the sounds of night crept into the cabin.

Friday morning came quickly. Caleb's bell clanged loudly throughout the quarters. This day was already planned to be different. I hardly ate my breakfast and I figured no one else had either. We stood at the edge of the fields under the watchful eye of Caleb and Claude who were present for the big event. I spotted two wagons coming down the paved road. The gang and hands all turned in its direction. The moment was about to unfold. The announcement concerning the fate of family members, field hands, women and children along with the bonds that the gang had formed with the hands and families were about to be broken. The deal of who was to be sent off had already been sealed. It was now just a matter of time to find out who it would be. I waited anxiously with Ressie standing by my side. The anger I felt Thursday morning watching Caleb beat Zeke would only escalate as the gang and me got ready to witness another one of the atrocities of slavery. Ressie squeezed my hand as a reminder of the spirit of our ancestors. My Aunt Raylene and my mother Paulene were depending on my strength and tolerance to guide the others.

The first wagon to come into the clearing was being driven by Ward. Bob sat at his side smiling like he had just closed a big deal at Peterson Industries. As they stopped Ward glanced at me but couldn't hold eye contact. He saw the look of discontent and anger on my face. He then held his head down as the gang looked at him; his body tensed with betrayal.

Our attention was now turned to the second wagon. A white man dressed up like a field overseer was driving. He had on brown trousers, a white shirt, tan vest, and a straw hat. The man sitting next to him was dressed in a black suit fashioned for this day and time. He wore a black coat and a derby that made him appear very distinguished. Remembering my history, I knew he was obviously a slave broker by the way he was dressed and the long and wide wagon that he rode.

My attention shifted to the two people riding in the back. Their backs were facing us. The gang moved in closer to Ressie and me. Kerry stood on my left with his family at his side. Lizzy and Kat stood in front of me with the two little girls in front of them. Aaron was next to Ressie and Rev sat on the supply wagon.

The man who drove the second wagon got down and went to the back of it. He motioned for the man and woman to get off. We waited nervously as the two bodies scooted forward. The terrible sound of shackles rattled and ran throughout the silent and motionless crowd. The woman stepped off first. She was escorted and held onto by none other than Ward. She was a medium built woman with broad shoulders, dark skin, full lips, and a broad nose. She seemed frightened by the hands that starred at her. Her breathing was very heavy and her eyes grew larger as she glanced around while surveying those making eye contact with her. Bob told Ward to calm her down, who without hesitation, started to shake the woman until she became motionless.

The white overseer waved for the man to get off. He stood and turned to the hands. The gang and I stood in awe. Even the hands were stunned at the sight of the man. It was as if the presence of a God-like spirit had been presented before our eyes. Never before had they felt the presence of any such human. He was absolutely magnificent. Even Caleb's beady little eyes opened, as he briefly looked intimidated. He was a brown-skinned marvel of a man standing about six feet six inches tall. He had dark eyes that hid under his forehead. His muscles were perfectly cut and detailed. But the thing that stood out the most was his hair. Locs were all over his head. There were small ones, long ones, thick ones, and thin ones. They were draped like a lion's mane, a king of some sort. I just starred at him in splendor. I knew he was the man - the unbroken African who carried the pure blood of the ancestors. The locs indicated that he was probably of the Masai tribe of what is now present day Kenya. The slave capturers had obviously gone into the interior of Africa to get this man. His sculptured physique entailed that he had to be part of the priest class or royalty that existed for hundreds of thousand of years. They were well trained in battle and educated in the arts and agriculture.

Kerry whispered to me, "Look at dose dread locs."

"Da white folks came up wit dat name dread. In Africa dey are called sacred locsand da Ka-ra-be-an de just called locs," I answered.

Bob stood up on the wagon and summoned Claude and Caleb to stand in front of us. He then said, "Listen up! My family and I look at this day as the dawn of a new era. The trades will make us a stronger family in the market."

I looked at Bob. I had heard this speech many times before. He talked as though it would give everyone some sort of relief.

He continued, "we have two new hands that Caleb, Ward, and my brother Claude will help adjust to their new home. I'm sad to say they come at a price. I'm sending one woman to New Orleans where she will work in the mansion and I'm sending two boys and a girl to work tobacco in Virginia. Now I don't want anybody to get upset because this new heifer and nigger is going to make us a whole lot of new young strong ones."

Bob gazed at the faces of the hands. The look of sheer fright was on the face of each woman who had both husband and children. I was praying that Raylene's prophecy of all seven of us returning could hold true. Even if it did, the separation of the hands would still affect us somehow. Claude and Caleb waited patiently as the crying from the hands started to grow. They turned to Bob who was still standing on the wagon like a king. He stood erect with both his hands grabbing each side of the lapel on the coat he was wearing.

He then yelled, "Take the woman to New Orleans!" Caleb and Claude started towards us. My heart began to race. Lila, Kat and Lizzy were in their sight. Claude raised his shotgun while Caleb said, "Com'on use Black wench. Use through makin suckas any howsz!"

It was Lila. She began to scream "K-ree! K-ree!" She fought and kicked while crying hysterically. Kerry lunged at Caleb but was met in the head by the butt of Claude's shotgun and fell to the ground. Lila momentarily broke free and held on to Kerry. It took both Claude and Caleb to pull her a loose. They took her over to the wagon, put her in, and shackled her wrist to a rail. Aaron and I helped Kerry back up. He had a large gash over his ear.

"No Kerry! No man! Please hold on!" pleaded Aaron.

But Kerry didn't listen. He yelled, "Lila! Lila!"

They both cried for each other. Caleb and Claude made their way back over. Claude had Kat in his sight. She began crying and screaming, reaching down as she held the two little girls close to her already sensing what was about to happen. Claude pushed her back and grabbed one of the girls all in one swift motion. She sat holding the other girl crying nervously. Caleb went over to Kerry for his sons.

Before Caleb could get his hands on them Kerry said, "No! I'se put my own boys in da wagon."

They stared at each other. Claude who was at the wagon with the girl cocked his shotgun.

"It's okay!" Bob yelled. "Don't let it be said that I don't have a heart."

Kerry took his boys over to the wagon. He put them in kissed and hugged them. The boys were crying not sure what was exactly going on. The blood and look on their daddy's face and their mother tied up in the wagon crying was enough to scare them. Kerry then hugged and kissed Lila under the watchful eye of the masters and overseer.

Kerry told Lila, "I'se want cha ta be strong in Nawlins. Member I luv ya."

"I'se luv ya too husband. I'se neva gon know a-nudder man da whey I'se known you. Take care of Iris," said Lila crying between words.

The distinguished gentleman shook hands with Bob. Caleb grabbed Kerry by the arm but Kerry, filled with anger and hurt, knocked it back and walked over to us. The wagon headed down the road that led off the plantation. Lila's voice could be heard in the distance still calling Kerry's name. He stood motionless with tears streaming down his face and blood over his ear as the faint sounds of the sweet and beautiful African woman he had come to know as his wife, the mother of his children, and most importantly, his friend, slowly faded away.

Bob then said to Caleb, "Go prepare the hand and Ward give that wench to Ressie. She knows what to do."

Claude stepped in, "Well don't just stand there. Git ta work!" He yelled.

As Ward took off the shackles of the lady, Ressie took her by the hand to show her to the cornfields. Lizzy followed. Rev comforted Kat and helped her up on the wagon. Kerry was devastated and barely walking through the rows of cotton as Aaron walked by his side for support. I stood there starring at Ward wondering just how we were going to pull this off with him. He looked back at me and for a second he seemed to have had a look of compassion. He then turned quickly and headed to the barn. We again were asked to perform duties in the midst of a traumatic event. I again pondered on the psychological damage that was being inflected into our minds.

Chapter VI

END OF THE BEGINNING

The afternoon continued as the gang and I tended to our work. The other hands were back to business as usual. Their experience of seeing this type of event helped them heal faster. But that was not the case with us of course. Kerry was pretty much out of it. He couldn't just cut his feelings off by picking cotton. Aaron stayed close by him, just a row over, occasionally glancing up to see if he was okay and not falling too far behind.

Claude and Caleb returned with the new man. They had put him in field clothes, but he remained in shackles. Claude said, "Caleb and I got bitness up at da house, so I'm puttin you in charge of this niggra," referring to me.

I nodded okay. Caleb got off his horse, whip around his shoulder and unshackled the man. I extended my right arm out to shake his right forearm, a gesture of peace in some African cultures. He stepped forward and locked forearms with me. Just then, in the blink of an eye, he turned around and caught the whip that was about to cross his back. It was as if he had eyes in the back of his head. He quickly wrapped the whip around his wrist and pulled Caleb to the ground in one swift motion. Caleb's attempt at initiating the new African to plantation life was a failure. Claude immediately drew his shotgun on the man, but I stepped in the path of the gun shielding my warrior friend, but scarring the hell out of Aaron and Kerry. Claude lowered his gun and laughed at

Caleb. Caleb got up frowning as the man tossed his whip to him inspecting him with contempt wondering just what kind of African he was, but reluctant to retaliate, Claude continued to laugh. He knew the next confrontation; he would have to show the new hand who was in charge. Caleb, feeling embarrassed got back on his horse, as the two rode off.

I didn't get much done in the fields it wasn't just the somber mood of what happen earlier that day, but more so training the new slave on the art of picking cotton. The day drew to an end and we headed for the clearing. Rev and Kat drove up with supper. Collard greens, hog fat, bread, and collard green juice was the menu for this Friday evening. Lizzy walked up with Zeke who had regained enough strength to attend dinner. He was moving slowly, but was receiving help from Lizzy who was his helpmate.

Aaron said, "Looks whose here."

We gave Zeke a warm hello breaking some of the tension from the day. As he made it to the table, Aaron just stood there looking at him at a loss for words.

Zeke said, "I'se gon neva regrets whad ya done taught me Aaron." Aaron reached to embrace Zeke who in turn raised his hand to stop him. "But I'se regret if ya hugg me now." We managed to smile, even Kerry with the heartbreak he felt, a sign of life shown in his face.

"Ressie told me whad happin to ya family. Das terrable fo a famly ta be sepraded. I'se sorry ta hear dat," said an apologetic Zeke.

I introduced the new man. "Ya'llcan call him Ma-say-e. Das da tribe I believe hees from. Soon doe dey gon give him a English name."

Lizzy repeated the introduction with the female. Her name is Camara, for now. The lady bowed her head appearing to still be frightened by all of this.

We sat there trying to eat but the day's events had taken so much out of us. Kerry and Kat stirred around in their food as Ressie insisted that they eat to maintain their strength. Iris ran up to Kerry and sat on his lap. He kissed her and began to feed his only remaining child. She saw the sad look on his face but did not yet understand what had happened to her mother and brothers. As far as she knew, they were just out on a wagon ride. I sat between Ressie and a teary-eyed Kat. Lizzy was finishing her supper I nodded for her to take Zeke and the lady back to the house while we finished our meal. Lizzy returned. We were all present including Ressie and the Masai.

I began telling them the plan. "Fuss of all none of dis can be repeated. I'se know Zeke is okay, but if he knows anythang bout dis, all Massa godda do is threaten to whup'em and he mights give in."

Then surprisingly Masai said, "Duz dis mean me too?"

The gang was startled. I stood quickly, afraid now that this brother may be broken "Hows ya know Englesh?" I asked.

"I am a prince from Africa," he said. "Bout a yeah ago, I came to you-rope (Europe) to do business for my family. I fell on disfavor wit some men who lader had me kidnapped. Day put me in de boddom of a very large boat, loaded wit rum, tobacco, and guns. We sailed to Africa I stayed in de boat for many days. Den day took de cargo off, and replaced it wit many African people. We lay on each udder for months, frightened. There were many tribes and many languages. When we got here to da place name Awlene. Da men dressed in Black paid fo me and da woman and bring us here."

We listened to the man, heartbroken by his capture and journey to the "New World." I realized he spoke English only for business reasons. He was not broken. I then asked him, "Masai?"

"Yes," he replied.

"Dis may sound crazy to you, but wees would like to pufawm a ritual. And in awdor ta do dat wees need da blood of a pure mind African man, likes yo self."

He looked puzzled. Ressie placed her hand on his and smiled. She said, "Is okay I'se meet cha in da mawning fo's ya goes to da fields." He nodded his head to affirm our request but appeared uncertain.

I began with the plan. "On Sadday mawining at eleven Rev when use and Kat stawds making yo rounds have some extra sacks in da wagon. When ya comes to collect da cotton stops fuss at da end of da cone fields. Lizzy, you dens come out and sneaks in da wagon. On yall's whey down here, Kerry, you and Aaron talks enough to brang Caleb ova and git off his hoss. Den ya'lls jumps'um and take um out I'se gon go fo Ward, Rev and I will den pud him in and we'll take off down to da cemetary." I checked out their faces to see if they were okay with this.

"Sounds risky, but I'se ready ta take dat chance," Aaron said. "Hows bout cha'll?"

Rev said, "Counts me in John, I'se thank wees got da Lawd on aw sides."

"Whad bout Claude?" asked Kerry.

"Claude neva comes down to da fields fo anythang sept announcemends and whippings," answered Ressie.

"Counts me in," said Lizzy.

"Me too," added Kat.

Masai responded. "I'd like to hep in all of dis," he said.

I didn't know what to say what answer to give. This brother was giving us his blood. I felt obligated to do something. Ressie then stepped in.

"Dere is sumpin use can do. When dey takes off in da wagon use make sho nobodys goes afta dem. Den use run

Nawth on da bayo da las few miles use needs ta run in da wada tills ya get to da caves. Waits till it's dawk and den comes out."

Masai asked, "Whey will I be runnin to?"

Ressie answered, "Use be running to da sound of da drums and whey da nights stawts ta get colda and colda, but only runs at night, and listun's fo da drum."

"Yo life will be in eva step dat ya take," I added.

He replied, "If I lose my mind, den I am dead already."

Suddenly the bushes rustled as an image of someone running was seen under the moon rays. We all knew it was Ward. I told the gang, "De plans stays da same, but it be a good idea Rev if use and Kat goes on up and keeps an eye out on dat boy."

Rev replied, "No problum, John."

Rev and Kat got up, said goodnight and left for the big house. We stood to head in for the night. Kerry was holding Iris who had fallen asleep on her daddy's shoulder.

A heartbroken Kerry said, "If all dis don't wuk den I guess I could make it here ta keep my promise to Lila and looks afta Iris. Night, ch'all."

"Night cha'll, I'se walk ya home Kerry," said Lizzy.

Aaron added, "I'se gon go now and git da new man in bed. Nite chall."

He took Masai and headed for our cabin. We had the extra bed.

Ressie and I stood standing as our friends headed in for what possibly might be our last night.

"John?" asked Ressie.

"Yes mam," I answered.

She sat back down and said, "I'se knows hows ya got here, and I'se knows ya haf ta make all dis come to pass I even knows hows ya spose ta gon home. But tell me sumpin baby? Where's ya'll come from? Dis 1999 place? Whas it like John."

I listened to Ressie ask questions that I really didn't know how to answer. She looked anxious to hear. I hesitated as she placed her hand over mine.

"Not dis time Ressie. Jus lisen." She sat puzzled, but anxious to hear. I began shamefully, "yeas from now, da white folks up nawt and da white folks down sout will have a big wah bout us bein free. Da nawt will win and Africans will be let go. Some of us will go back to Africa. Da res will stay. Some will have been here too long and won't know nudding else. Dose dat stay will have nuddin to stawd wit but dey will leave da plantation any howz. Da res of dem will stay and take whad eva Massa give him. Den fo bout a hunnard yeas, das a long, long time from naw, you know? Wees gonna look like free people and live on aw own plantations, but thangs will still be wrong. Till one day, a strong African woman, jus like you Ressie, will say she don't wanna ride in da back of da wagon no moe. Dat she wanna ride up front. Dat will stawd a big uprising dat last fo awhile. Dey will call it da rights movement."

"Da whad?" she asked.

"Neva mind, Ressie, jus call it da time da ancesta's heard aw cry. Dese times we will fight hawd so wees can eat in all da big houses wit'em, dranks out da same well, even use da same out houses. We will go whey eva dey go, eat whad dey eat, ack like dem, and talk like dem too."

"Whys would ja fight hawd ta not be like yo self John? Don't make sense ta be likes da one dat calls ya uh nigga?" said Ressie.

"Well Ressie," I said, "White folks won't calls us niggahs or beat us hardly any more. Dey will does it anudder way; through sumpin dey call da sistum."

"Whas a sistum?" she asked.

I tried to explain to the eager Ressie. "Is like gon into Massa's house, cuz he said das whey ya got ta live, and all da rooms in da house gots a diffrunt kind of baddle dat ya gooda fight. Das a sistum. Dat's when ya godda beat da sistum, and dens you

can hav da thangs dat you wuk hawd fo; da same thang Massa has."

"I'se confuse John. Whys would ya go into da house in da fuss place? I thought ya said dat ya had yo own?" Ressie asked again.

I smiled at my wonderful aunt and continued. "When wees fought to get whey Massa wuz, some of us Africans fogot whey wees come from. Now we stuck in Massa's house and his sistum but don't realize dat weez stuck in it. And some of da ones dat stayed back is waitin on Massa and some of us Africans ta come back and git em. Da rest ain't wadin, deys mad, so mad dat dey killin each udder. Dey figa wees ain't comin ta hep um cuz dey black. So dey stawds to hate de selves, stawd doin thangs ta look and ack like Massa, so maybe folks can look at um and treat um diffrunt. Deys don't understand de is a part of another sistum. Its so crazy dat dere ah white folks dat da massa's done put in da sistum too."

Ressie remained curious. She then wanted to know about the rest of the gang, "Wheys yo friends at in dis 1999?"

I said, "Well, Rev is tellin Black folk dey can have riches and all if dey put dey trus in God, cep he don't tell em dat da whey Massa got it fixed. Evabody can't be rich and since most Black folk is caught up in da sistum, dey only see riches and powa like Massa. Ward is like a new kind of Caleb, he don't whips ya, but he still trained ta do anythang Massa tells em. Lizzy don't trust no man, cuz mos of um done been

broken by da sistum, da rest is like Ward. Kat and Aaron, de sings, but only about Black folk killin each udder, takin off dey clowes and havin de whey wit each udder. De calls each
udder niggahs and whenches in dey songs."

Ressie's look revealed a sad face. What she was hearing from me was unbelievable. I continued on. "Kerry wuks on one of da bigges plantations Massa got. He runs, and jumps, for lots of money, mo money den lots of white folks got. Sometimes folks like Kerry does good thangs, bedder dan mos, but Kerry don't know his self eder. He makes lots of babies like he is a breedah, cep in 1999 dere ain't no mo breeding gone on."

"Wheys you at in all of dis John?" Ressie asked looking with a concern that I would not let her down.

I answered, "I'se whad you call conchuss, Ressie. Dat meant I'se knows whas gon on most of the time. But I stawded off like Ward and Kerry. I lisun to da songs Kat and Aaron sang. I even lisun ta Rev and knew women like Lizzy. But I found out bout myself and Massa. And I'se don't blame Massa know mo, not in 1999. Sees, I'se ask Massa in da uprisin fo my rights, den I ask him ta lets me read and write, den fo a good job. Massa gaves it all ta me and when he didn't I fought him fo it, and I won. But ya know Ressie? God still didn't fully bless me. Acks me whos I am? Wheys did I come from? Whyz I here? He said I didn't make you John, just whad are you any hows? You sho ain't no man of mine, use just like da res of um. Den I prayed and acks him fo hep ta know my tru self and hav wisdom. He blessed me, so I went back to git da res of da field hands, cep since I'se been here dese seven days, I knows now whad God also wands me to do?"

Ressie asked, "Whas dat baby?"

"He wands me ta gits.....da house hands too, including Caleb."

Ressie nodded her head as though she understood. I hadn't realized it, but I was crying. I never had to explain anything in this fashion. It all seemed so clear. I now knew why I had come back. It wasn't about saving or loving a few conscious and African-centered people, but the unconscious ones as well, the way I once was. I looked at Ressie.

She smiled, "Naw das some powa-ful story."

I couldn't help but laugh a little thinking back to my comment Sunday under the oak tree. I said, "Specially if da ancestas has anythang ta do wit it."

"Tell me one mo thang baby," Ressie asked. "If we done been acksin God befo 1831 up until 1999 ta hep us, den maybe wees acksin fo da wron kinds of hep. Maybe God don't wanna give us all da same thangs Massa got. Maybe sum of whad Massa got ain't dat good in his eyes."

"Ya know Ressie, I'se read many a book dat done taught me a lot and ansad lots of questions. But whad you said is da bes I eva heard. Black folk done walked off da plantation but some de lef they mind sitting in da qwadas."

Just then the horse could be heard. I said good nite to Ressie and ran in. As I lay down I noticed that my roommates were asleep. No sooner than I could say my prayers I heard someone whispering my name, it was Rev. Aaron, Masai and Zeke were awaken by the disturbance.

"Whas happnin Rev?"

He said, "I'se ova heard Ward tellin Bob and Claude bout aw plans up at da big house kitchen. Den Kat walked in and acks dem could she go down ta da bayo, cuz one of da lil guls done run off. Probably ta looks fo huh sista dat got sent away and das whey she might be. Claude tells huh ta gon on. Den he drank some mo whiskey dat de wuz already dranking and den takes out afta huh. Says he gon teach huh a lesson. Da whey he laughed and looked, dere sumpin up John!"

I didn't hesitate to think, "Go get Kerry and de udders. Masai watch da trails; Aaron use come wit me."

Kat told me later what had happened at the bayou before we arrived. It was dark when she got near the bayou. The only source of light was from the full moon in the sky. Its reflection off the murky bayou water added a little extra light to the trail. She arrived at the big tree where the little girls usually played. There under the tree in a stream of tears was the girl she had come to adore. The child reminded her of one of her own back home. She was shivering and scared. Kat assured her that everything was going to be just fine. The child explained naively to Kat that she was scared to go back because her sister was gone and they might take her away from her and Iris and the little kids and grown-ups she knew. Kat gave her a shawl that she had brought to keep her warm. Then Claude rode up and startled her. She thanked him nervously for letting her come look for the girl. He tipped his hat and gave a treacherous smile. Kat was very scared; it was dark and she was thinking what Ward might have said. Little did she know how right she was? He got down off his horse and stared at her and the girl. Kat held the little girl tightly reminding Claude how late it was and how she had to get up early to prepare breakfast for him and his family. Claude inched toward her removing his belt, laughing sinisterly, showing his tobacco-stained teeth, while his breath reeked with the smell of whiskey. Stepping back Kat began to beg for Claude not to hurt her and the girl. He said the girl was not who he wanted and that he had heard she wanted to be a big woman and bring down his family. He lunged at her and looped his belt around her neck stating he was going to have a little fun with her. The girl was frightened and began to cry. Claude ordered her to sit down, shut-up, so she could watch him. He then threatened Kat that if she screamed, he would kill the girl, tie them to a rock and throw them in the bayou. Kat knew she couldn't risk the girl's life. She nodded to Claude as he tightened his grip. He began to justify his actions by telling Kat he knew she wanted it, that he had seen her smile at him and his brother, and watched the way she walked around the mansion. Kat told me that she began to feel guilty and reflected on all the explicit and sexually oriented lyrics she had sung. She remembered the skimpy clothes she had worn. Her intentionally flirtatious ways and how she had daunted in front of hundreds of men much to the dismay of her parents. She saw the girl look on to see what was about to happen to her thinking of the times her parents and I had told her to set better examples for her daughters. Claude then told the girl to remember what she was about to witness. That's when I came up.

"Da only thang dat shes gon see is yo head blown off!" I said standing there pointing his own shotgun at him. "Thought cha neva wents no whey wit out yo shotgun. Dis a bad time fo you ta fogets it. Naw git off hur. Gits off huh now!"

Claude let Kat go. She dropped to the ground crying helplessly. He tried to make a move to the horse for a pistol he had in a holster. I cocked the gun freezing him in his tracks. The gang arrived with Ressie, minus Ward. They looked in disbelief but Rev had already told them something was going down. They quickly put things together.

"Rev and Kerry gon git Kat. Lizzy, grabs da girl," I said. They began to console and calm Kat. Lizzy gave the girl to Ressie. I gave Aaron the gun and told him don't hesitate to shoot.

"You stupid nigger. Don't you know what's waiting on all ya'll? Huh?" said Claude. "Ain't no son gon kill his daddy boy!" laughing with the stench of whiskey on his breathe. "Pauline and I was in love and you was created right here under dis tree," he added.

The gang was stunned and confused. Claude's accusations held them dumb- founded. My anger grew as we stood face to face. I thought about what he said being under the tree with Pauline. Visions of him raping her took over my mind. He wiped the grin from his face, changing into the face of a mad man.

"How bout it boy? You man enough to kill your daddy?" He said, spitting tobacco on my shirt.

I lost it. I quickly grabbed the belt he was holding looping it around his neck and got behind him all in one motion. Claude fell to the ground as his efforts to break free became futile due to his drunkenness. I raised my head to the sky, starring at the full moon never looking down, as I tightened the grip on his neck. The gang watched in horror.

Rev yelled, "No John! No! He ain't worth it."

"Shut up Rev!" Ressie shouted. "Das a time fo eva thang! Kills da devil das kills my sistas."

I stared up to the heavens unconsciously listening to the gang yelling at me.

Claude started to gasp slower and slower for air, his drunken body growing weaker as my grip became stronger. He made one last attempt at separating my hands from the belt, but failed. His spirit had left...

Aaron yelled, "He's dead man!"

"John enough! He's dead!" shouted Lizzy.

Kerry moved in quickly "John! John!" he said trying to separate my grip on Claude.

Ressie spoke calmly. "Let him go John. Deys free naw. Deys both free and so's you."

I released the death grip I had on Claude. His lifeless body rolled over. It was done. My plantation father, murderer of both my mother and aunt, the horrendous overseer who had just attempted to rape the girl I had always known as my little sister, was dead. I turned to the gang who was starring at me with fright. I was sweating and breathing rapidly. I then looked at Ressie. She nodded her head assuring me that now was the time.

"It's okay John. You can tell'em," she said.

"Tell us whad?" asked Rev.

I told my friends while I stood looking down at Claude's body, "Many yeas ago three sistas comes ta dis plantation: Paulene, Raylene and Ressie. Raylene wuz da fuss to have a child from an African man. Das hows use got here Lizzy. Massa Ugusta had his way wit Raylene, she gaves him two chillun's, das Kat and Ward. Befo dat he tried to have Pauline, got drunk and passed out, but his young sons Claude and Bob (they both barely into puberty) brung huh down here to dis tree. Bob helds huh down while Claude has his way wit huh. Das hows I come to be. Later on Claude has my momma beaten and hanged cus she tried to run off wit me and Aaron. Den last Sadday he made my Aunt Raylene drank some poisun and when dey burred huh at noon, we got here."

"Hows long you known dis John?" Lizzy asked.

"Since Sunday Ressie told me. I'se didn't figa it be a good thing to tell ya'll at da time. Ya'lls might be wit Ward right now," I answered.

Kerry added, "Use right. If ya would have told me dis Sunday, I'se be at da big house wit Ward right now."

Kat and Lizzy starred at each other briefly then embraced. Knowing they are truly sisters, they humbly vowed never to criticize or think badly of the other ever again. Just then Masai ran over. "Somebody is coming," he said.

I knew it was Caleb. I told Aaron, "Hide de gun and horse, Kerry help me move Claude. Da res of ya'll back trail to da qwadas."

Kerry and I pulled Claude's body into the brush near the edge of the water and kneeled down as two men rode through in a wagon. It was Caleb and Ward looking for Claude. As they rode on by, Kerry glanced down at Claude's body. He was finding it very hard to believe that he had witnessed all of this.

I asked him, "Aw ya okay Kerry?"

He answered, "yeah man," patting me on the back. "Are you okay?"

I assured him, "I felt like Claude lef me no choice. Dis animal was not jus gon rape any ol woman hees bout to rape his half sista."

"All dis is so crazy man," Kerry said, "Jus thankin dat Ward, Kat, Bob and Claude all Massa Ugusta chillun's is wild."

Kerry and I headed back to the quarters. I began praying asking God for forgiveness for what I did as I lay there still shaking and nervous from my actions. My stomach babbling and burning like hot stew.

Aaron rolled over and whispered to me, "It's jus like Ressie says dere is a time and place fo evathang John."

Maybe it was justifiable in a biblical sort of way, an eye for an eye, but I couldn't relax or just sleep this feeling away. Claude was still human. Never could I have fathomed the thought that I'd ever be able to kill.

I stayed up all night, as the morning came quickly, the aftershock of last night was my only thought. I knew Claude's body would be discovered and I had prepared to take full responsibility for my deed. At the table one would have expected a better feeling about making it home today, but it was just the opposite. Everyone was nervous, frightened and not eating. This whole ordeal could backfire and turn into a permanent nightmare. After nibbling on our food, we headed to the fields. Rev showed up with the supply wagon and news.

He said, "Dis mawning Massa Bobby asked Kat bout Claude. She didn't quite know whad ta says so I stepped in and asked Bob had Claude made it in from town cuz das whey he told me he wuz goin."

"Howd he look?" I asked.

Rev answered, "He seemed peculuh bout it. Den Kat tells him Claude passed huh downs by da bayo las night and tried ta take huh inta town but she had da gul. I'se believe he didn't buy it, cuz Kat whad'nt doin too good when she says it. So Bob sent Caleb to town and told Ward to look afta us."

"Don't matter too much if Caleb gon ta town. Might makes it easy ta get to da cemetary. Make sho ya keeps an eye on Kat," I replied.

Lizzy then saw Zeke who was back at work. As he started for his row she ran up to him and gave him a big passionate kiss and said, "Zeke, I'se neva met a real honest man befo til I'se met you," she then ran off to the cornfields.

Zeke was stunned and overjoyed. He had a grin as wide as a row of cotton. He yelled, "Aaron! Aaron! Di ja sees dat! Huh?"

Aaron insincerely smiled and hugged his friend. He said, "Congradjulation Zeke," very sadly. He knew that in a few hours Zeke's world could change with the loss of Lizzy him and the rest of the gang.

Ressie came up while the others went to the fields. She pulled out a small jar and said, "Dis is da blood das ya gon need. I'se also put a lil well wader blessed by da ancestas."

"Thanks Aunt Ressie," I said, then curiously I asked, "Wheys did ya get da blood of da African woman?"

She smiled pointing to herself. I was surprised, but I guess I really shouldn't have been. Ressie had never told me anything about a husband or children not even an encounter with one of the masters. I asked, "Use neva been wit a white man?"

She answered, "Knows I had not baby. My only child, a gul, wuz takin wit huh pappy to Cal-lin-ah. He wuz a field hand. I'se thanks bout huh all da time. We named huh an Ah-free-can name, but rounds Massa we called huh Fait (Faith). I'se lost my peace when she lef, tooks me awhile to git it back."

I was glad to hear that a white man had not touched her. My faith in getting us back seemed like it was possible. I stashed the jar in my cotton sack and joined the others in the fields.

Kerry asked, "Hey John, whad wuz you and yo Aunt Ressie talkin bout?"

"Ressie gaves me da blood we need ta git home," I answered. "And da woman blood is from huh, cuz she ain't neva been wit a white man."

"Das great," added Aaron who was listening to our conversation.

I added, "I'se also found out she had a husband and dauda, but dey wuz sold off to Cal-lin-ah."

"So's ya had ja a lil cuzin, huh John?" replied Kerry.

"Guess so, says huh name wuz African, but dey calls huh Fait rounds da Massa and nem."

Aaron responded, "das cool ya know? Having two names an all in dese times. Thank dey means da same thang John?" he asked.

"Don't know Aaron. Maybe, maybe not."

Kerry added, "Maybe it means da same thang like dose African Kwanza days at Christmas?"

Aaron replied, "Man jus git back ta wuk."

I was picking my row and then it hit me. I stood and looked around another piece had been added to all of this.

Kerry was concerned. He asked, "Use okay man?

Aaron added, "Whas up John?"

"Git back to ya row so Ward don't get spicious bout us," I told them. "Sumpin came ta mind. Ressie's gul name fait is da same as Imani in one of da African languages. She said da gul wuz takun ta Cal-lin-ah. Naw, Miss Imani back home is from da Gula Islans off Sout Cal-lin-ah. Says she named afta a great ancesta. Dat musta been Ressie's gul."

Kerry asked, "Howd she end up in Buffalo Hill?"

"Miss Imani said dat da spirits tolds huh ta come ta Buffalo Hill cuz she had some roots dere as well"

"Some helluva roots too," Aaron added.

We picked our rows glancing at the sun every so often waiting patiently and uneasily for noon to arrive. I wondered about the murder, Aunt Ressie and Miss Imani, our fate, and most importantly how Rev and Kat were doing. Was everything okay? Were they on schedule? Was Caleb going to come riding up with Claude's body? I kept working anxiously.

At the house, Rev told me later that he and Kat prepared lunch for the Petersons. Bob came into the kitchen and wanted to know had Caleb and Claude made it back yet. Rev told him no. Bob grew even more suspicious. He told them to hurry up and serve their food so he could head to the fields to see what was happening. Rev hurriedly served them. He had taken Claude's pocket watch from his coat the time read ten o'clock. They went out back and took the supply wagon to the barn, put in some extra sacks and then headed to the well to fill the buckets. Rev checked the time it was ten-thirty.

As they approached the cornfields the female hands dumped their baskets row by row. As they got to the end where Lizzy was she came up out of the tall row to dump her corn. The other ladies returned to their row as she stayed behind drinking a cup of water. She turned to Rev who was watching her back. He then signaled her on board. She delved into the corn and Kat assisted her by covering her up. They both were nervous and scared, and rightfully so. The horror of the past two days had begun to take its toll. After seeing Zeke whipped, Lila and the kids being taken, an attempted rape and a murder that had to be kept quiet, these ladies were barely keeping their sanity. The tension began to flow even thicker. Rev checked his watch. It was eleven. They headed for the cotton fields as I saw them approaching, I grew anxious. I signaled Aaron and Kerry to get ready for a diversion when they arrived at the edge of the rows. Everything seem to be going well, too good to be true. We would only have to distract and subdue Ward, since Caleb and Claude were not around.

Then the bad luck began. As Rev neared the edge, I could see Caleb approaching in the distance, Rev came to a stop. I signaled for Kerry and Aaron to hold up. Ward saw Caleb also. As we waited, our plan began to unfold before our eyes. Suddenly Caleb slowed down looking toward the bayou. He rode off on the trail, more than likely he had spotted Claude's horse. This was our chance to break. I was getting ready to pounce on Ward when Bob came riding up from the mansion. The gang and I became concerned. I could feel my heart pounding faster. Butterflies were in my stomach. Bob stopped in front of Ward. He had a shotgun strapped to the horse's side. Rev motioned to me that it was eleven fifteen.

Bob asked Ward, "What's going on here? Where's Caleb and my brother?"

Ward answered, "Caleb wuz riding up den he took off downs to da bayo. Don't cha worries doe. I's got evathang unda control here. Gots um all in line Mista Pederson."

Bob turned and starred at the excited house servant Ward. He was clearly frustrated at all of this and became even more agitated by Ward calling him Mr. Peterson. The cheesy grin on Ward's face was quickly erased by the look in Bob's eye. He rode up closer to Ward. We became attentive to the confrontation of master and want-a-be.

Bob began in on Ward. "You are neva allowed ta call me anything but Master! And you ain't in control of nothing because none of these niggras has dumped their cotton in the wagon!" He hesitated catching his breath, while the hands and myself began to dump our loads. I had managed to keep the small jar by not dumping all my cotton in the wagon.

He continued at Ward. "You are a gutless idiot, who will never surpass the status of the trained monkey that you are. So, don't think you are in control of anything. You don't piss unless I say so. Is that understood?" Bob eyed Ward as if he had cursed God himself.

Ward was humiliated, hurt beyond words. All the admiration, respect and loyalty he held for his boss wasn't worth a damn. He glanced at us in disgrace while Bob looked down the road for Caleb. I knew Ward was hurt. I wished that I could have talked to him a long time ago. I could have shared personal insight regarding corporate America. Explaining to him it was about get and gain which was aggressive. There was no love in the boardroom and never go to the table without having the guts to be yourself. I felt sorry for him, but I knew this was a hard lesson he had to learn. His appetite for glory and recognition in this type of fashion, though it can have its reward, but only renders one spiritually and morally bankrupt.

Silence prevailed for a second but was suddenly interrupted by the sound of a charging horse and a screaming Caleb. In that instant everyone's face changed. Bob watched with confusion as did Ward while Caleb continued to yell out words that no one could yet make out.

The hands stood in confusion as the gang and I knew that Caleb was riding with the news that could possibly seal our fate. Caleb neared as his words began to ring clearer.

"He's dead! He's dead! Massa Claude is dead!" He yelled pulling up and nearly falling off his horse after making the animal stop suddenly. He was completely out of breath, panting hard, trying to collect himself and explain exactly what his yelling was about. We listened with caution knowing that anything he said to connect us to Claude's murder would result in our immediate execution.

Breathing heavily, Caleb began to tell Bob, "I's found Claude unda da big tree down at da bayo."

"What the hell are you talking about Caleb?" Bob asked angrily.

Caleb raised his head from being bent over trying to catch his breath and said hesitantly, "he's dead Massa. Yo brudda is dead."

"That's a lie! My brother is not dead!" He then yelled out, "Caleb! You and Ward keeps an eye on these niggra's." He turned to Ward. "Dis is yo big chance to prove yo Black-ass is worth something." He trustingly tossed Ward a shotgun then took off to the bayou.

Ward nodded his head ready to assume leadership. I glanced at Rev it was eleven thirty. I signaled for Aaron and Kerry to move in on Caleb. He was weak, tired, and was leaning on his horse, not paying any attention, thinking Ward had his back. They sprung quickly, pulling him down, and wrestling him to the ground. Kat hopped off the wagon to get his whip and tie him up. Ward then jumped down and pointed the gun at Aaron and Kerry.

"Let'em go!" Ward yelled.

Aaron and Kerry obliged, not trusting this brother at all. Caleb broke loose and charged at Ward, snatching the shotgun and knocking Ward down. He cocked the gun, aiming it at Aaron. As Caleb fired Masai then jumped in the way. He shot Masai in the arm, but Masai kept coming knocking the gun out of Caleb's hand, swiftly grabbing his neck, and snapping it with a monstrous twist. Thinking fast, I grabbed the shotgun beating a stunned and scared Ward to it. All the hands watched in horror, not knowing what to make of this. They all began to run towards the quarters. Lizzy came out from under the sacks in all the commotion. I pointed the gun at Ward.

"I killed Claude las nite cuz he killed my momma and my Aunt Raylene. He tried ta rape Kat. Naw it's time yo ass wakes up and smells da coffee. Use coming wit us wedder use likes it aw not," I said angrily.

Ward knew I meant business. As we all hopped in the wagon, I looked back for Ressie. She was nowhere in sight then I saw Masai standing, holding his arm. All the hands had run off except for Zeke. He just stood there frozen, in shock not knowing what to say or do.

Lizzy saw him. She said, "Zekes, I godda go. I'se godda git oudda here. Use runs away ya here! Burn it down and runs wit Masai to da nawt, Zeke." He looked confused still not speaking. She added, "Please Zeke, doos as I says! Don't make dis hawda dan it already is."

All the supplies had been dumped, I then asked Masai, "Use okay?"

"I'se can still run. Gits oudda here! C'mon Zeke les head fo da bayo," Masai replied.

"Wese got twendy minutes John!" shouted Rev.

We took off as fast as the two horses could take us. We went down a rough road that led off the plantation. I glanced back to see Masai and Zeke running in the direction of the bayou. I also saw Bob riding up fast. We rode off the plantation and headed for the cemetery up on the hill. We were about a quarter mile away. The road became steep and the horses grew tired. I looked back and saw Bob turn off the plantation heading towards us. I glanced down at the jar of blood that I had holding it tight so that it wouldn't fall out of my hand from the ride of the rickety wagon. Bob was gaining on us. I could see the cemetery's gate. Suddenly, we heard a shot come from Bob's gun. The horses became confused and spooked off the road making it hard to ride on.

"Git off!" I yelled. "Wees go haf ta make a run fo it!"

Rev brought the horses to a complete stop. As I jumped off the jar of blood slipped out of my hands and broke on the ground. It was unbelievable. The gang took off as Bob fired another shot and got closer. The wind started to blow fiercely. We were about thirty yards from the cemetery. The sun had disappeared; it had become dark as the wind picked up. I ran behind the gang making sure we all made it. They were yelling, crying and praying. We were all out of breath but would not stop literally running for our lives. The sound of fear was in every stride we took. It was as if I could hear their thoughts begging God to save them promising to change their lives around from the materialistic, immoral, and unethical institutions to which they had succumbed. As we entered the gate the wind blew heavily. There standing at the grave of Raylene was Ressie. I checked back for Bob. I could see him in the distance. Suddenly a bolt of lighting hit spooking his horse throwing him to the ground. I tried looking through all the debris of leaves, grass and branches that were being tossed by the wind to see if he was moving. I turned back to see that the gang had formed a circle at Ressie's request around Pauline and Raylene's grave. A black cloud hung over our heads. We realized it was the same cloud from the ceremony. Just then the wind calmed down to a steady breeze, but a somber cloud remained.

I said to Ressie, "I'se dropped da blood."

She reached into her sweater and pulled out another small jar of blood. "I'se thought it be wise if I saves a lil bit," she replied.

I took the jar of blood, dipped my fingers into it, and put a drop on everyone's forehead in the circle, including myself. I then poured the remaining in the middle of the circle on Raylene's grave. I turned back to Ressie.

"Fi minits John!" shouted Rev.

I began to say good-bye to Ressie. "I'se got ta thanks ya fo heping me and the gang find aw selves. I knows we can finds aw peace now in 1999. Fos I go doe, dere is sumpin I godda tell ya. Back dere in 1999 da is a woman dat heps me ta stay strong and smawd bout African people. She's da one dat tells me I wuz to come here. She came from da place in Cal-lin-ah whey huh ancesta's lived. Huh momma gaves huh da name of a great you-ra-ba ancestor in Cal-lin-ah named Imani that means Fait. I believe dat wuz yo daughda Aunt Ressie."

Ressie was overwhelmed with emotions; with her hands covering her cheeks, tears began to flow. I hugged her and smiled.

"My baby gul made it!" she cried.

I replied, "And she had chillun's dat taught da ways of da ancestas too."

Rev then shouted, "One minit John!"

I joined the circle holding Kat's hand on one side and Ward's on the other.

Then a shot was fired; it was Bob, apparently surviving the fall.

"Ya damn right one minute, I ain't gonna give ya that long," he yelled. "Break tha circle!"

I yelled to the gang in the midst of the angry wind authoritatively, "Don't break the circle! Please don't break it!"

I could feel Ward resisting my hand. I squeezed it tighter and said, "Dere ain't no promotions and advancements here my brother."

He hesitated, then no longer resisting, turned to Bob and yelled, "I'se quit!"

I looked back at Ressie. She had both hands high up in the air. "Neva forget yo ancestas," she shouted.

Bob then tried to fire a shot, but the gun was empty, he lunged at us to break the circle. Suddenly with the power that only God could produce came a loud thunderous noise followed by a lightning bolt out of the black cloud that hit the middle of the circle. We were floating in total darkness again with the sensations as before. Silence so deafening we couldn't hear ourselves breathe, unable to speak, we traveled through haunting images of African people of the past. In our minds we saw them floating down a blue river surrounded by lush forestry, building pyramids, marching across the desert, running though the jungle, sitting and crying in a dungeon, lying on top of each other in a ship. We saw ourselves working the fields of Peterson plantation, slaves running with Harriet Tubman, some hanging from trees, the Klan riding, Marcus Garvey waving from a car. We stood on the street as Tulsa burned down. We sat on the bus with Rosa Parks. We stood in the crowd when Malcom was shot, on the balcony as Martin was gunned down. We saw a neighborhood in Philadelphia bombed. We stood on the side of the road as James Byrd was dragged.

Suddenly, I could hear myself breathe, the dim voices from the others trying to speak. A light began to appear; the ground was now under my feet. We opened our eyes only to be blinded by the afternoon sun. As we looked around people were hurriedly moving around and talking. We were back in 1999. We saw each other, the gang still holding the token gold shovels they had been given; all the fake jewelry , Nike's, wigs, tatoo's suits clothing the entire look we left with was back in place. They momentarily were stunned that we had all made it back, before they realized that it was true, I looked sternly observing them. I said, "Unless we remember, we are doomed to repeat it."

They immediately slammed the shovels down. Aaron yelled, "Yes! Yes!"

"Praise God!" shouted Rev

They all celebrated screaming, jumping up and down, praising God and crying. I too could smile. The people present at the ceremony stared at us not knowing the reason for our jubilation. They could only wonder if we were exaggerating the moment of the groundbreaking event. Indeed it was, if they only knew. Somehow the journey of lessons had come to an end. I turned to see Bob walking up to us with the media behind him. As the flash bulbs popped and cameras rolled, the confrontation began again along with the strange celebrating going on behind me. Bob starred me in the eye and said, "I believe I need to reconsider some things."

Starring back I said, "Now that you know the truth, I think you do."

"I'll be in touch," he said while extending his hand for a shake.

I hesitated looking at his hand. "Not yet, you know how to find me," I said.

Bob nodded to affirm our promise. He then turned his back to me facing the media. They began to inquire about our little meeting asking him what does that mean and what does this means?

He raised his hands to calm them down. Then he announced, "The theatre project is cancelled!" The media frenzy escalated.

I turned back to see the gang joyously head off towards their limos, their families, friends and entourages. The media was going berserk with news that the groundbreaking ceremony had been cancelled. News reached the camp of the protestors; I could see the celebration of victory. I stood there for a couple of minutes listening to Bob shock the hell out of the other board members.

Camara, my co-worker from the center came up to me smiling. "We did it Ra! We did it!" she shouted. She stayed on my arm as we walked towards the protestors' camp. While passing a TV crew, I heard an announcement.

"Although the national weather service has just confirmed that none of the weather radar devices picked up any disturbances whatsoever, we have live footage of strong tornado-like winds that lasted exactly seven minutes," said the newscaster. I laughed a little, thinking of the spirits and power of our ancestors. As I got closer to the camp, I noticed a figure standing at the back of the protestors. As friends patted me on the back, kissing and congratulating me my attention was caught by a woman. It appeared to be Ressie. Wiping my eyes for clarity, I got closer and realized it was Miss Imani. I gave her a big hug first before I said anything.

"Hey Miss Imani."

Starring in my eyes she responded, "Hey baby I want to know all about your journey."

"I think you already know most of it," I replied.

We paused for a moment. Then the smile she had became a curious expression. "You saw her, didn't you Ra?" She asked.

Hesitating for only a few seconds, I answered, "Yeah.... I saw her, I saw them all, and they were strong, beautiful, African people, just like you and me...cousin."

She began to cry in the midst of the yelling and jubilation and asked me, "What did she say?" wiping back her tears and sniffling.

I turned back to the crowd with Miss Imani at my side as I repeated her words, "We must never forget them-and never let the circle be broken."

Miss Imani and I headed to where I was parked and drove back to the Southside. I stayed up the entire afternoon and into the evening telling her the details of my journey and about our ancestor Ressie and her sisters. I explained the changes we went through and how I hoped the others would remember the lesson of it all.

Miss Imani was in complete awe and said, "you have been blessed by God to have been through such an ordeal. God has put the value of spiritual and educational leadership in your heart. You must answer to your calling during your journey in the body until he calls you home to the realm of the ancestors."

She told me this while I was sprawled out on her couch. The last thing I remember her saying was tomorrow would be the first day of the rest of my life. I had finally found the first night of peace in seven days.

The morning arrived and I headed across the street upstairs to my apartment. It felt great to take a hot shower and drink a cup of my favorite coffee, yet I had the strangest urge to go to Rev's church. I didn't go against my instincts, I had learned from both Ressie and Imani to trust them.

I went to the church arriving near the end of Rev's sermon. Even though I was standing in the back, Rev noticed me right away. He continued his sermon.

He said, "I know it may sound cliche, but I had a dream last night." Laughter came from the congregation, as I even felt the humor. He continued, "I was visited by our ancestors of Buffalo Hill, African ancestors to be precise. Because of what they told me, and what I saw, I have an announcement to make. I am going to start a series next Sunday for the next few months. Afterwards, I will extend the teaching alongside Bible study. All members will be required to attend. The series and studies will be outlined with required reading. We'll study our history and contributions of the Nile Valley civilizations as introduced in the book of Genesis. We will study Black history before the Bible, in accordance with the Bible, the origins of the Bible, the translations of the Bible, the doctrines, dogma, and denominations adopted by man. The concept of Christianity existed long before Christ in the institute of spirituality that Christ came to reaffirm and why we are not taught it in that manner. We will tell you of the Africans who survived that we give no honor or remembrance to. Their strength, hard work, and sacrifice in the days of their blood being spilled in this strange country. We will explore and identify the institution of self-hatred and why we have so much of it. We will cover the plan of Willie Lynch on how to make a slave and how that plan is still in effect today and alive in our minds!"

Rev went on to add, "And if any one of you are afraid to go there with us, then I say to you after this service - never return. Because now is the time for this church and other churches to become liberated. This is the dawning of the age of enlightenment so go where you can hide from us. But, I must remind you that you can never hide from who you are and what you are. We will create ministries to help those answer their dreams, manage their lives and lifestyles from money to marriages while living in this Western culture."

Rev then eyed me. Smiling, he continued. "We will embrace all African people in the spirit of Malcom when he said, before we were Republicans, Democrats, Liberals and

Conservatives. Before we were Christians, Muslims, and Catholics, we were Black. We are not here to promote anything other than your understanding of who you are, where you came from, and what God wants you to do with your life."

"You see, to revisit the past and learn your history is just like a marriage that needs counseling. To work out their differences they must discover and admit to the history of their problems. They just can't forget their past and start anew thinking everything is going to be fine. No! No! No! They must go back and deal with the genesis of their problems in order to live and go forward. Any good marriage counselor will tell you to keep others out and only let them see your strengths." This new leap is not about segregating anyone of us from anybody based on race, religion, sex or political persuasion, no Sir we are not about that. This is about integrating our history into our studies and being better able to apply some of this information into our lives to let us go forward with blessings. We need to study and investigate certain aspects of our history to better understand if we are repeating past mistakes; philosophies that are outdated; traditions that we may need to reclaim or throw out. We need to do an honest in-depth critical analysis of this thing we call Christianity. Let the church say "Amen".

He motioned for the congregation to stand for prayer. The choir sang and church was dismissed.

As I headed out the door towards the parking lot, I was both moved and glad that Rev was now ready to attempt to teach black people some truth and spirituality. He would be teaching their history and mission in life. I knew he would receive criticism from other ministries - so did Dr. King. The experience he had in the past would give him the strength to go forward. Listening to him reestablished my belief that the church has, is, and must always be the pillar of strength for the African community. Politics, economics, and education can never be separated from it.

Just then voices called out my name. I turned to see the gang looking surprised, "I said, Hotep! Brothers and sisters! What are you all doing here?"

Elizabeth said, "We went by your place last night but you weren't there.

"Yeah, Rev told us to come on out this morning," said Kerry.

"Yeah, He told us he had a special message to give," added Ward.

Kat asked, "Where were you last night? We were worried."

"I fell asleep at Miss Imani's house after telling her of our journey," I answered. "How's everybody doing?"

Elizabeth said, "Well, last night we stayed at Rev's and talked about the journey, our experiences, and how our lives must change. We all realized now why you fight and work so hard for Black, excuse me, African people. I realized how Zeke changed my life forever. I saw the genesis and the process of black male destruction. It's time black women and men understand that the legacy and process still exists. We must stop blaming others for our problems. Presently, we are the co-conspirators in our own destruction. So I am going to start some sessions on relationships and teach them about the law as well. But, "Mr. Center Director," I'd like to conduct it at the center."

"Done," I replied. She gave me a hug.

Aaron then said, "First of all, Kat and I are going to stop rapping negative lyrics. We may team up sometimes with some positive artists to help shed a positive light in the hip-hop community. I mean you can only be a gansta, hustler, playa, and a "balla" for so long. I was lying in most of my songs anyway, besides my parents didn't raise me like that, I was just attracted to it."

Kat added, "Aaron and I also agreed to change our first names, we hadn't decided which ones yet, but adopting African names with our American slave names, remembering both the free African and the enslaved ones, like you John; I mean Rasidi. And with your permission, we would like to merge Rev's youth group with yours over at the center. We want to teach them things like gender respect how to stop using the N, B, an H-words."

"Done," I said hugging them both.

Ward stepped out. "My turn," he said, as we all laughed. "The experience of the journey taught me that corporate America is on a whole different level. I realized John excuse me, Ra, that your leaving the corporate world to work for the struggle and liberation of African minds was your calling. But, I am groomed for corporate America I believe that African people need to be a part of all professional institutions and systems. I strongly believe that we need to prepare ourselves for corporate careers, as well as, creating our own. I plan to launch a program to help black college students prepare for corporate America, something I found out the hard way. I want to tell them how not to get lost and not to be a sellout to themselves. I, too, would like to do this at the center, as well as putting it on the Internet."

"Done," I replied again, with the gang laughing at my continuous reply. Ward and I shook hands and embraced.

Kerry then began on his experience as Rev walked up from shaking hands. "My experiences of the journey taught Rev and me that we could make a bigger impact on African people, simply because we have the admiration and respect from the people and community. We have the attention of the media and the finances to promote and make change in our communities. Rev and I are going to form a partnership to promote black people across this country to join a group or organization that is positive in their communities. We plan to get athletes, ministers, teachers, politicians, and parents to help carry it out. And, on a personal note, I will apologize to my three children and their mothers. I want all my children to know they are a family. And, I am going to make a vow before them that I will be a better father." Kerry bowed his head, raised it up slowly and said, "Lila and the kids taught me so much. I feel I need to do this and pray for a woman I need, not just one I want."

Kerry and I embraced, as did Rev and I. I hesitated, smiling then jokingly with a plantation accent, I said, "So's ya'll tries ta run me oudda bitness huh?" We all laughed. I then said, "Seriously now, I can't express the feeling of joy and love of the spirit that is before us now. Miss Imani told me last night that crazy as it was our time in slavery was allowed by God. We needed to go through such an ordeal. You have all learned your gift. You've realized you're calling and will extend it to help others around you. As Ressie would say, that is so wonderful."

"The essence of all this is not that we are not just Africans in America. We are God's children first and to be recognized as that we must first learn to love ourselves. Then we can live as the commandment, "Love thy neighbor as you do thy self." We have to teach everyone to be significant."

Rev said, "Amen. Now since you're reciting commandments, I guess you won't be a stranger," pointing back at the church. We shared a final laugh Rev then asked "Who told you to come to church this morning?"

"Ya'll did!" I answered. "The blood of the pure African man and woman was a symbol of the resurrection of the true spiritual mind that bonds us all together. The journey taught me that I was wrong for calling you Sambos, and for that I am truly sorry. Education is for some, self-education is for all."

I said my good-byes and turned to my car. Before I got in, Aaron yelled, "Hey Ra! Just who is Sambo anyhow?"

I smiled and waved a peace sign. "None of ya'll."

"So yeah Horus, a journey of lessons that took us seven days to find ourselves was somehow wrapped up in only seven minutes. During this past week each one of us had spent a couple of days over at the center. I had a chance to spend sometime with each one individually and we talked about the journey in detail." Horus turned off the tape.

"Well...that was some powerful experience you guys encountered," he said. "Tell me John, do you feel the gang may backslide and become bitten by the so-called "Western Bug" again?"

"I don't think so Horus. I get the feeling that the journey was like the movie "The Ten Commandments" when Moses came down from the mountaintop, hair gray and all. The people immediately knew he had seen the Almighty. That's kinda like the feeling I get about the gang and me. We've been to the mountaintop. History and the future looked us in the eye. Everything is so clear now you know? I now have this great unconditional love for my people and the answer to all our problems lies within our minds, our subconscious conditioning is keeping us so locked down. Apart of us must go back and rediscover. We must honor and understand the struggles of our past and present generations in order to go forward with the spirit and determination they possessed even in a time of despair and atrocities." Our history is not just of kings and queens; inventors and the first this and the first that, but a magnificent spiritual system that branched out to the world. That system is what keeps you looking ahead

"And what about Bob?"

"Who knows?" "I know he never has lived up to his family's full expectations. Maybe Bob can also somehow come to terms with his family's history and move on in the spirit of truth."

"And what about the other European-Americans? Where do they fit in all of this?"

"It's like I always say Horus, concerning America's dirty little history until she can fully deal with her past: publicly apologize for slavery; settle any due reparations; and have a totally serious discussion about the racial divisions within her borders, this country will never heal. The children whom this country continues to bear will continue to fall victim to this ugly institution. It reminds me of the story of Esau and Jacob at war while in the womb. Its America's womb that is cursed, because the parents are cursed."

"You are by far the most spiritually educated person I know John and I'm going to get this story printed as soon as possible. I have one last question though. Do you think the races will ever come together?"

"That's one for the ages, Horus. But you know if we make up our minds to deal in spirit and in truth, anything is possible. We must first understand and know that there is no race! And you ask will we ever come together? I say we never separated, we just believe we have, and so it is."

Chapter VII

THE ROUND TABLE

A s Ra and I continued our talk on the state of people coming together, the gang walked in. Saturday morning
was spent at the community center where they had been initiated. They promised their ancestors and themselves they
would spend weekly services there.

After a round of hugs and greeting from the new family,
I asked them each for a personal statement of their experience and how it affected them. I didn't have to ask for vol-
unteers, everyone seemed anxious to talk. So I decided to
start on one side and go around the room. Rev insisted Ra
make more coffee. The first speaker to appear was Aaron. I
marked Aaron's name on a blank cassette, popped it in the
recorder then gave him the go ahead to start.

"Looking back at what I experienced last Saturday has
given me a new outlook on this whole hip-hop game. I can
clearly see how our music is really being "played". You know
what I'm saying. I mean it's like nearly everything that's hitting the airwaves ain't talkin about nothing, but sexing somebody up. The brothers are saying things about the sisters that
really ain't that cool."

"Such as," I asked.

"I mean," Aaron continues, "very few songs say anything
that's positive about our sisters, calling them names, having
them appear half naked on videos, on CD covers or in concerts. And what's unfortunate the sisters are responding too!

This whole thing has become a multi-million dollar machine that dictates what kind of lifestyle you should take on. I mean some folks abandon their mannerisms, their diction and vocabulary, and adopt a new kind of slang. I have heard some deep southern accents try and sound like they're from Brooklyn. There is also a certain kind of walk, the jewelry that you should wear a whole new generation of clothing and how you should wear them, not to mention that most common folks cannot even afford them. So bills go unpaid to buy hundreds of dollars of clothes and sneakers that equates to about only three days of outfits."

"The attitude is probably the worst because you have some people like myself who were raised in a house that promoted good morals, education and some holistic values, but now are trying to be "gangsta" or hard. These people don't even smile when they take a picture. It's like to smile or laugh or get-along with people is taboo. Like, don't' even go there. It's' like I can't' let anyone know the real me because being myself is a sign of weakness or you are just simply out of touch."

"Why do you think some of these young people reject authority so much?" I asked.

Aaron ponders for a second. "Well, that's a good question. As well as I believe the hip-hop community needs to take more responsibility for the images we project and the words that we say. I also believe that one-third of the problem is that we don't view authority or leadership the way our parents did."

"Why's that," I asked.

"Nearly all of our lyrics are a manifestation of what we see and hear and it is safe to say that those in authority or leadership help create that type of environment."

I asked sharply, to describe these figures?

Aaron responded immediately without hesitation as I has finally asked the question he has been waiting for. "It's a reaction to the complacency of some. 'I got mine you get yours attitude', bougee black folk the 'I don't have anything to live or die for' 'po black folk' and also the 'pick yourself up by the bootstraps' kind of attitude so we can all be rich and get along."

"Elaborate!" I quickly said.

"I believe that these Mogols have lived up to their creed that it's all about money and nothing else exists. They really don't care what you say about each other, they know that music is your stage to express the self-hate that you have for one another and this is why groups and artists like Public Enemy, Common, Dead Prez and the other conscious rap-artists get shutdown from the airwaves and videos because of the fear that black folk might wake up and see who the real "balla, playa, pimp and gangsta" really is."

"The parents and the community that have achieved a "so-called" economic respectable position often leave the community, which is OK to some extent, but never returns to help others achieve or understand certain values to succeed. Not really knowing that their kids are the ones who most likely to be more loyal to the whole hip-hop game. Parents think that moving away removes what we hear. This is your bougee type."

"Then you have the so-called "ghetto type" the kind that think and feel that this is just the way it is. Yet even in their hopelessness and disparity they still manage to buy Air Jordans, expensive jewelry, hip-hop clothing, hair weaves, expensive purses and nice cars through assistance programs. I mean here you are complaining about life in the community and there's a Lexus or Escalade parked in front of Section 8, HUD, or housing projects."

"So you're saying that a portion of the problem is in the home?" I responded.

"Exactly," Aaron said, "Now be mindful that I believe that we all have a hand in this. The recording industry is the conspirator, but the parents also allow this at very young ages. The community, church and school leaders who only talk and hope then just try and pray this thing away."

"Hip-hop is not a culture. Culture is to cultivate, to nurture, and to make change to better a group of people in their civilized lives and community. It is the expression of the soul that helps the group achieve its goal of prosperity."

"Rap music is a reaction to a social situation that has gone awry. It is the expression of what the mind has perceived through the continuing conditioning of self-hate among our people brought on by the constant lacking of institutions and vehicles not created by us to see ourselves different than the way others see us. Thus, we were called niggers in the past and we have not fully understood who and what we are. We have evolved to accepting the word so casually amongst us. Ra explained to me that the word 'nigger' in its original meaning, breaks down to 'one who is stingy'. One who is stingy has something another person wants. So we must have had something the European wanted to call us that name. Now why we say it takes on a whole different meaning. Yet, this is clearly what happens when we don't study. Forty years ago you fought inequality and said what's happening "my brother or sister," "my king/queen," "my comrade" in the struggle with positive and strong greetings. Even if we were poor there wasn't a great economic rift between us. What little we knew of ourselves, let us keep some dignity and self-respect? Now forty years later we have more jobs, more money, more education, more opportunities, but yet we greet each other with "What's happening my nigger," "fool," "dog," "G (gangsta)," "ho's" and "bitch-es." If there is a message in all music, then what are we say-ing that's different."

"So we are the co-conspirators of our social ills?" I asked.

"Absolutely!" "For example, look at priorities in the home most parents or single parents work like hell to achieve something that they say must be in order to maintain a life and this is with a kid or two. Compare that to their college uneducated mother, father, or grandmother who probably raised five or more kids on necessities and values and life was considered "as the good ol days", there was always love, caring and understanding. Nowadays even these broke-ass folks are killing themselves to try and have something mate-rialistically to show that life is good and the children pick this up and carry it with them into adolescence and have a spoiled mentality. I know this because I was like that and I rapped about the ghetto that I never saw and things that I never experienced. I'd rap about the things that I got and things that I wanted. I can afford to act and you can't so that's why you envy me kind of attitude. You hate me as a matter of fact you are a "hater". So I'm saying if parents and the community are genuine and sincere with the so-called nega-tive words, images, attitudes and lifestyles of the hip-hop community, they want to do away with. Then reach back for what most of us already know, which was given to us by our elders and ancestors. Give us the spiritual and moral values that you had rather than trying to work hard at giving us the material things that you never had, in essence, which had no value at all. And that's why we don't rap about spiritual val-ues and morals, but of the physical and material values the things that are given and presented to us."

"Amen!" I shouted with a smile, "How does Zeke play in all of this?"

Aaron sits quietly with his head bowed down, the gang looks solemn too. As he sits down, he leans forward in his chair. He grasps his hands together as if to pray.

"It's OK brother," Ra says.

Aaron now feeling the support he had on the plantation raises his head and answers. "I always thought that slavery should never be talked about, it's as if it's embarrassing to discuss. But I'm trying to choose my words carefully so that you may know how truly I feel about what Zeke gave me. He gave me what I said, what we should get from our elders and ancestors, because Zeke is an ancestor now. He taught me that life is still not to be judged even with its lack of equal distribution to all. We are well endowed with a spirit that feeds us what the world can't or will not give. Zeke only wanted to achieve knowledge he knew would set his spirit free even in slavery. Here I am along with others enjoying more freedom than Zeke could imagine in his wildest dreams and I didn't have the faintest notion to know anything."

Aaron puts his head back down. "We are so messed up as a people and we know this. We have to find the time to be a family; parents, grandparents, aunts and uncles the elders have to tell the story. These parents in all their madness of their jobs, lifestyles, and commitments outside of the home, have to commit to talking and spending quality time with their children. Some parents spend more time with their lover than they do with their spouse or children, and most homes have more movies and television sets than they do books. If there are any books, they are bought mostly by women about love and relationships. Zeke helped realized the importance of knowing self; only then can you help your family and community. And that's what I plan to rap, write and talk about."

"Ashe! My brother," Ra said.

"Ashe!" The gang added.

I leaned over to my recorder to announce my next speaker, Katherine. Ra handed Aaron a cup of coffee along with a nod of approval for his statement.

Katherine cleared her throat then begins. "Aaron covered some things that I too would like to add. First, I believe that we have to remember our ancestors and our living elders in the home and community. Ra gave me a book to read called "Of Water and the Spirit." It's about an African child who is taken away at five years old to a Catholic Jesuit School and taught the ways of the European. He later escapes after fifteen years and no longer remembers his language and very little of his family and village life, although the image of his grandfather is embedded in his dreams which helped him get by during those years. Upon returning to the village he had to be initiated back into his true spiritual self and his culture."

"As African people in America we have also been taken away but now have an opportunity to get back into our true self. We can no longer expect to prosper spiritually looking out of the eyes of someone else. Our language, spiritual system, self value, self-worth and love for each other was taken away on the plantation, the auction block, the slave ship, the classroom, the job, and in some cases like Aaron said in the home."

"Those girls on the plantation taught me what true motherhood was about? First, there can be no casual sex, or unprotected sex. This is not just about catching a disease, but a disease of not being ready for motherhood."

I flaunted and flirted my way in, out and around the record industry, concerts, videos and wild parties. This is not an image for a mother of any kind. The lyrics I used displayed sexuality, foreplay and grinding. I promoted my behind and vagina as the key to being a strong black woman. I always had something to bring home to my daughters; a T-shirt with a rapper on it; designer clothes for tots and children; and an explanation why I wasn't around."

Once I came from a show only to be late to my daughter's birthday party. When I walked in the music was playing loud and they were listening to an uncut song."

"What's uncut?" I asked.

"Raw, with profanity." "My oldest daughter saw me and said look mommy! With excitement and enthusiasm in her meek little voice she had her hands on her knees half bent over, smiling at me, slightly off rhythm while the song said 'you's a fine _utha _ucka won't you back that ass up'. At that moment something went through me, but I quickly ignored as everyone was smiling and clapping as if this was a rite of passage that I had passed on to my daughter. It was the same smiling, clapping, excitement, and enthusiasm that my fans gave. The other women I rapped about were jealous of me because of the way I worked the inside of my vagina, which was better than theirs. My diamonds and jewelry are not fake and cost more than any amount of weaves or horsehair that any Asian could sell. My blue, pink, gold and blonde wigs were bought especially from designers and high — — — salons. I ignored her because I had become the desire of so many men and their fantasies. I was everything that I wanted to be, everything that the industry and society said I needed to be."

"I realized now that the reason I ignored my daughters was because I was trying to deny what I had become. To make her stop would be for me to stop as well. She was only mimicking me because a daughter should be like her mother. I don't even believe in half the things I sing about. None of those lyrics represent my true self they only represent my conditioned self."

"I need to be a mother first and foremost. I need to teach my daughters about womanhood. I will show them that giving that much energy, time and spirit into a fleshly appearance is not womanly, godly or African. It should not be your culture and it should not be a reflection of your soul."

"My experience on the Peterson Plantation taught me the value of motherhood. It is what I will sing about. Lauren Hill sung of her son Zion. I too shall follow in the tradition of those sisters who sing of strength about a woman; family and how various experiences help them grow."

"Is this your pledge to the community?" I asked.

"Yeah"! "Absolutely"! "Just this morning I had my daughters show some other girls how to make a bow and placed it on their original "good" hair. The one the Creator gave them and made no mistake in doing so. I taught them that everything about them is beautiful because they are a woman, a black woman that does not need a lot of powder, make-up, hair pieces, wigs, false eyelashes, eyeliner, lip gloss, bras to push up their breast, tight clothes to show their figure, alcohol filled perfume to destroy their beautiful skin and the approval of any man whose intentions are not just. They need no breast enhancement or any form of cosmetic surgery they are beautiful just the way they are."

"Although I will be teaching this at the center I plan to follow through with as many parents as possible and I will call out their number."

I looked puzzled. "What do you mean their number?"

"They have a role to play not just at their jobs and in society, but in the home. There is no excuse not to participate in an event or be a part of where you have sent your child to gain knowledge or get an education. All of these so-called educated African Americans with degrees and letters behind their names should be ashamed to have kids participating in programs or schools and they cannot behave, read, write or address an adult with respect."

"And what of the black folk that's less off?

"That's easy Horus! Most of them who are at home should really be involved. They also should be the ones - that Aaron mentioned who don't have a lot of material wealth - that should instill values, spiritual meaning and morals into their kids because it does not cost them anything. Again, there is no excuse for your child to behave rudely towards adults. Any kid that does and continues to do so, then I would say follow them home and see the real problem."

As I rattled an ink pen against my teeth, I then asked Katherine, "So are you ready to turn in fame, fortune, all those fine fellas and fans, to help reeducate some black kids on what to expect from their parents who may not consciously even give a damn?"

Kat looked at me with a blank stare as if I struck the very nerve she was trying to get rid of. "All I can do is try. And with the experience I had on the plantation with my ancestor; I know that the majority of the young girls that come up under me in the spirit of my ancestors and the Creator will prosper and be quality women and mothers."

I nodded my head affirmatively, "I know that they will."

"I would like to add," says Ra, "that nobody blames the hip-hop community for all our failures in society. Simply put, if the music has failed, it's only because the environment has failed the community has failed, which means the church has failed and without question it must mean the home has failed."

The gang responds with Amen, Ashe, and a "I heard that!"

I stopped the tape and turned it over as Elizabeth prepared to speak.

"I know I never could have in my wildest imagination dreamt of how I could come to understand how to relate to a black man. Aside from falling in love with myself and getting to know me, I now realize that to love a black man takes a love that is unknown even to the man. The African American male cannot always get into his woman. It is his woman that has to get into him to bring out of him that which he cannot always connect with. His spiritual strength is the key to the family, prospering, but he must know the foundation sits on the woman. I know whole-heartedly now that we can't continue to just relate to one another, 'I need you to complete "me" attitude.' It is obvious that the man and the woman must eventually succumb not just to the knowledge of oneself, but to the knowledge of what are an African American male and an African American female role in this country and sometimes the world. The stereotypes and generalizations of who and what we are, as well as, how we are supposed to love one another." We need to be mindful of the labels and beliefs and just be souls, the light that shines within us that happens to be of African ancestry. I have something here with me. I seem to take my briefcase with me everywhere I go.

"As long as you got good stuff in it", I replied.

"These are papers that I read to the adults at my weekly relationship class. It's by a sister I found on the Internet at World African Network. I'd like to read it to all of you."[2]

By Michelle N. Jackson
Willie Lynch may have provided the foundation for the institution of slavery that controlled Africans during slavery, however African Americans are the people who continue the tradition of dehumanization discussed

2 Michelle N. Jackson/Commentary: After Willie Lynch 6-30-98

in his writing, "Let's Make a Slave: The Origin and Development of a Social Being Called 'The Negro'."

The formula Lynch provided is the same method used by individuals outside our culture, to control African Americans today and the same method employed by African Americans to control and manipulate one another.

As we journey toward the complete healing of our minds, bodies, and souls, we must realize and correct the actions that continue to stunt African American growth and prevent our healing. The process of African American rebirth encompasses the need to understand what has been done to us, and must include an introspective approach that acknowledges the wrongs we do to ourselves.

First, let us look at the violating acts performed by whites against blacks.

The process introduced by Lynch discussed the breaking or seasoning of the Black male. He says in the writing, "When it comes to the breaking the uncivilized nigger, use the same process [used for horses], but vary the degree and step up the pressure so as to do a complete reversal of the mind."

Lynch then explicitly explains the violence he believed was necessary to break the Black man, "Take the meanest and most relentless nigger, strip him of his clothes in front of the remaining male niggers, the female, and the nigger infant, tar and feather him, tie each leg to a different horse faced in opposite directions, set him afire and beat both horses to pull him apart in front of the remaining niggers." Lynch continues, "The next step is to take a bullwhip and beat the remaining nigger male to the point of death in front of the female and the infant. Don't kill him. But put the fear of God in him, for he can be useful for future breeding."

This process first shattered the mental stability, and fiery spirit of the African man then negatively affected the African woman and child. It is evident that any human dehumanized and killed in such a violently insane manner does not only traumatically destroy the person killed but also utterly destroys the family. It creates a perpetual sense of fear in all witnesses, which will always exist unless conscious efforts are made to bring about change.

Practices that embarrass and dehumanize African people in this so-called civilized country still exist today. Just a few years ago in Jasper, Texas a Black man was tied to a truck and dragged until his body was torn completely apart. We must not forget the white man who burned and beheaded a Black man in Virginia. The killing of these men is a part of an American tradition of installing fear into Black people locally and nationally. Once again, Willie Lynch's plan manifests itself in American society.

In breaking the African woman, Lynch makes it a point to break her spirits by committing the previously mentioned acts in her presence. However, he takes it a step further to ensure "good economics". He says that role reversal will occur when the lynch style killing of the Black man is performed in her presence.

Lynch explained the method when he said, "We reverse nature by burning and pulling one civilized nigger apart and bull whipping the other to the point of death—all in her presence. By her being left alone, unprotected, with the male image destroyed, the ordeal caused her to move from psychologically dependent state to a frozen independent state."

Lynch goes on to discuss the cyclical affects on the Black family, "In this frozen psychological state of independence she will raise her male and female offspring in reversed roles. For fear of the young males life she will psychologically train him to be mentally weak and dependent but physically strong. Because she has become psychologically independent, she will train her female offspring to be psychologically independent as well."

Fear is one of the most controlling emotions and it is continually used to manipulate Black people. The installation of fear from watching lynchings creates fearful women who rear their children in fear to create a group of people who are motivated by fear (thus the cycle is created).

For example, many times Black people move out of African American communities because they fear being killed, robbed, or terrorized by their own people. By leaving Black neighborhoods, our collective power decreased which benefits white America. The fear Black people instill in one another and we eliminate the fear we have for our own people. This is the point when African Americans become the perpetrators of the cycle.

Once writings like Willie Lynch's are publicized, those who are exposed to them should initiate plans to break the cycle. We must realize that we are the makers of our destiny so if we continue to act based on fear, we are allowing others to create our future and inevitably our demise.

Black women have to stop raising their children in fear. Black boys must be groomed to take on the responsibilities of men in a family setting and be trained to be warriors. Young Black girls should be taught to be co-leaders of the struggle of freeing the Black nation and not independent beings who "don't need a man". As Black women cannot take on an attitude of "false" independence because we need Black men to co-lead in the struggle toward liberation. The violence among ourselves also has to stop.

These are the ways we have learned to repeat the injustices committed against us during the seasoning process and endearment of slavery.

We must recognize the game that is being played and the ways in which we willingly participate. Our continued mental enslavement will never end unless we take responsibility for our role in its continuation. Take time to understand the psychological affects of slavery so changes can be made.

If freedom is our destiny, work must be our responsibility!

"When I saw this, it was as if I was reliving the journey all over again. This writing has everything in it that has happen to relationships that I not only experienced but those of my friends too. It is also what I experienced with a front row seat in living color watching Zeke being humiliated and stripped of his manhood because he believed in our love."

"Before that Saturday I looked at African American men as most of my friends looked at African American men from a biological and financial standpoint. There were also concerns of how many kids he had. We never talked about the inside or the full spirit of the black men at least not in depth. We would often describe brothers by their status. For example there was "oil man" (he worked for a oil company) there was "Lexus man," there was "suit man," we even had a name for a brother that had slept with two of my friends we called "Mr. Two Good."

There was never a time a name or reference to something spiritual. After sometime I really don't think we really knew any of these brothers' real name."

"I had always measured guys by this model I had created. It measured his background, wallet, career, was he a father, how many friends he had and did he hang out a lot. How often did he like to go out? Did he spend a lot of time away from home? What kind of relationship did he have with his mother? He had to measure up to this while worshipping the ground that I walked on. Because my position in the legal field, my Benz, my good looks, and what I had declared as heaven between my legs was more than any man could imagined." Some of these things are okay to ask and know, but the spirit-side of it I never sought.

When I arrived on the plantation I met Zeke and saw the other hands in that situation. Seeing how they were psychologically and spiritually broken, I could not help but feel sorry for most of the brothers I have dated and heard about through my friends and court trials."

"The African American man still harbors a psychological ill effect from slavery. The information that I plan to teach in my relationship class concerns post-slavery syndrome. Even after three hundred and eighty years my experience dealing with my brothers along with seeing them on the plantation only confirms this. My relationship with Zeke and seeing what he went through to please me and make me proud to be called his wife was emotionally overwhelming. I know that I still carry the spirit of his love for me. During this past week I got a call from a friend who I had brushed off because unlike other guys who wore suits and drive expensive cars, this brother didn't own a suit and drove a late model Jetta. Out of all the guys I knew he was the only one that called and offered his concerns. He told me that he had won an overnight stay at a Galveston Hotel and that it was mine if I wanted. He said he knew it wasn't Jamaica, but it would give me a chance to get away. We talked for a while and during the conversation he asked if I needed any help at the center. I realized then that this brother also has the spirit of Zeke. I could feel that he had never been intimidated or threaten by my status. He made me feel like it wasn't his outside that I was getting but the inside, his heart that it was okay for me to know his spirit. It seemed as though that is what he was offering me nothing more, nothing less, but his true self."

I knew at that moment that Zeke was in both of us.

I smiled and asked "So....a brother got a shot at ya! Huh?"

Lizzy and the gang laugh. "Still not just any brother," she replies. "Ashe"! I sipped my cup of coffee and turned the tape over to start the fourth interview.

The gang sat with the look of intrigue on their faces anxious to hear each other's story.

"So my brother," I said, giving Ward a coy look. "You were the resident "house Negro."

"Yes, my name is Ward B. Shaw and I am a recovering Negro." Everyone laughed. It was obvious Ward was a family member who had taken a long hard road home.

"This journey that I took with my brothers and sisters actually began long before last Saturday. My Negroism started like mostly everyone else. I finished school and college; I wasn't from the ghetto and grew up on the Northside. My parents were considered well off, which means they had good status. I made the grade, the honor roll, the dean's list, and was recruited by Peterson Industries. I was adamant about telling everyone I had made it. I assimilated into the corporate lifestyle on and off the job. I would have never guessed that I had been miseducated, not by what I had learned, but by what I hadn't learned. Just the other night Ra and I were talking about how we both were recruited and what was given to us and how it changed our lives. He understood my point of reason and I understood his as well. He had been there longer than I had and he told me some things from a perspective that I had not seen before. I did not sell out to my people as much as I sold out to myself."

"I went into the corporate world hook line and sinker, and it was easy because I had already been conditioned to take the bait. This is the American dream, high school and a college education, a well paying job with a Fortune 500 company, my own office, corporate card, the whole works. As a house Negro like my ancestor would say, "where am I gonna go that's better than this. I became lost in it all."

"The corporate life gave me a high, a rush, it was exhilarating. Yes, it was aggressive it was about get and gain there was no love in the boardroom. There was just the love of business."

"When I occasionally walked through the areas where the line worker or the blue collar type were they looked at me with their names sewn in their industrialized uniforms. I knew I was better, smarter and richer than they were, and they knew it too. Nobody called them "Mr." around here. I was drowning in this box of illusions. I had the credentials. I must be better than they were, they had no college education and they had no letters behind their names. They knew I didn't sweat. Hell yeah! I was better. This was the American way and everything on paper was what I had earned. I had a reputation."

"In all my arrogance and knowing and the things that I thought I knew and all the things that I thought they didn't know, the one thing that was a fact is, I didn't know myself."

"I still believe that there is room and a place in corporate America for the African in America, let's be real here, we can't all be entrepreneurs and run businesses. I believe that there are those in corporate positions who missed their mark or calling to leave and help create or start businesses of our own. Many people gain that experience to be able to leave one day and do just that. College and high schools train us very well to work in a structured environment and follow task and assignment that helps us earn a living. But after seven to ten years working in a corporation, you should be able to make a living and know how to interact with people."

"The ancestors knew this. Their way of doing business was simple reciprocity or fair trade. We are by nature an agrarian (agriculture) people so we knew the principles of fair trade and doing business. All of this is in our spirit, mind and body and we have to maintain a sense of communalism and fairness, because black folk have a tendency to shy away from black businesses. We must also keep in mind to believe in prosperity, but not to think too highly of becoming "stupid rich" off of our people. If for whatever reason you do, you thank the ancestors, show reciprocity, and give back."

"This experience really educated you that much on how to treat our people?" I asked.

"Yes!" "You see first we've got to realize like myself that we've been mis-educated. Carter G. Woodson's book "The Mis-education of the Negro" is a pinnacle book on the mis-education of Africans in Americans. He comments in the book about the Negro and his slave mentality that his conditioning is so strong that when he approached the back of the house to enter, if there is not a back door he should make one. Unless we can learn or recondition ourselves to shape, create and mold our own reality, there will be more and more Ward B. Shaws coming up."

"What was a defining point for you on the plantation Ward?" I asked.

"Well Horus, I put a lot of faith in Bob to save me from Ra and this terrible transformation. I realize now that it was all blind faith. Somehow I knew as hard as I tried I could never really be accepted, but my conditioning was so strong even in the face of danger even when I was humiliated and embarrassed. When he told me that I would never surpass the status of the trained monkey that I was, I still thought that I could win him over. The defining point looking back at this was the belief that my brothers and sisters still believed in me. Although Ra told me that was the only way we could get back, I believed I still could be saved; and saving myself was definitely the defining point."

"So from here out my work is to instruct and teach my people about the western capitalistic business culture and entrepreneurship. Teach them not to just think about making money first, but have a love of desire for what you do. Develop good relationships with the people and you can bet the prosperity will follow."

"The way my ancestor Ward sold out to his people and the gang was because he had been deeply conditioned to do so. I too had been deeply conditioned, but I'm here now to makeup for him and myself. I have the blessings of my ancestors now and I know I must make a difference, Ashe!"

Ward receives a round of applause. Kat and Lizzy both get up and kiss him.

Next up on the interview was Kerry. He seemed delighted to want give this interview.

I put in a new tape and told Kerry to go for it. He obliged.

"First I would like to settle something that came up while we were walking down the path to the plantation the first day we arrived concerning my job."

"Oh Yeah!" said Lizzy. "Was that about the players giving in to the strike?"

"That's the conversation," Kerry replied. "I want to say something on the matter concerning the business side as well as the lifestyle that comes with it."

"Professional basketball is nothing more than entertainment just like movies and television. We are nothing more than athletic actors on a stage. Just like any other celebrities we have roles to play that pay very well, better than most, but that does not make us any more conscious, politically aware or an expert on matters of race. Most of still don't get it on how to manage and control our own money. I was accepted early in the draft, the promise of fame and fortune was something I practiced year around to achieve. I deserve my place in the elite because I worked for it. I understand where Ward is coming from with that, but it took something traumatic for John to be shaken at Peterson Industries. If it was not for his elders and their knowledge of his family and faith in him, he may not have become who he is and as we know him to be. We may very well be calling him John and not Rasidi."

"The comment I made concerning my loyalty and trust to my agent and the people who were there to make sure that everything was in place was done out of appreciation because I could not do it alone. I didn't feel as though I could trust my people because my environment where I came from never told me I could. It wasn't until after this journey that I realized I was living in a conditioned state along with the same people who were also conditioned. I associated money with white people, to me they only asked for what I was con-tracted to give. My people asked for what they thought I owed them, simply because they looked like me. Yes, my team relations department taught me to say no to certain people and organizations. They told me not to affiliate with any political or religious cause that was labeled by the league as detrimental to the league's integrity, as with any job. So I say that to say this, if I had known then what I know now things would be different. It is only now that I can start to make a difference."

"So how do you feel about your lifestyle now after your experience with Lila?" I asked.

Kerry took a deep breath. A father, who had lost his fam-ily, quickly replaced the look of confidence he showed, defending his position as an athlete.

"I still haven't gotten over how she cried for me as she was going down the road. The other day, as I drove by the

Peterson's mansion, I could still see the road as the wagon took her away. I...I... cried. You know.... I have met so many beautiful black women; I even had my share of white ones, being in two, sometimes three cities a week. It becomes routine the way these women act. They come on to you so eloquently and charming, but deep down you know they ain't nothing but ho's and whoochie's; all of 'em, black and white. They then become nothing but objects to fill voids of desire and pleasure, just more trophies to put on that sexual shelf. Most of them know there is no future in a one-night stand. I mean.... You know it's just routine, to see them at the arena exit, the hotel lobby and the nightclubs."

"What happens when they tell you that you are going to be a father?" I asked.

"You surely don't feel good Horus." I mean you know it's going to be a burden on your career. You play the game that she trapped you and then ask yourself - uh ... is it yours? Your agent tells how much to offer her and you are told it's best not to have any contact with her, just send the money. It's kinda like breeding on the plantation. Massa still continues taking care of us and telling us what to do, even with our kids."

I asked him, "Do you still plan to unite your kids and the three mothers as a family?"

"Yes, if the ancestors say the same." My kids have moved up to number one in my life. Basketball is still important to me, but it doesn't rank in the top five categories of my life. It is only a vehicle to help my people and community."

"Do you think any one of these mothers has the potential to be like Lila? Or is Lila still yet to be found?"

"Maybe, I don't know really. There would be so much reeducating them I guess for me to lead by an example of being a conscious African American man and father. The mothers may not be ready to give up some of the things they enjoy about western culture. I mean I did meet them in hotel lobbies, clubs or at the arena. As for 'a Lila', I guess I would have to just trust the Creator and my ancestors or the gang." Kerry points at the gang and smile.

I pondered with my pen, flipping it back and forth. I looked at Kerry's eyes, knowing his smiling with the gang is only a front. I saw the hurt was still in Kerry.

"I feel as though there is something else you would like to say about Lila, but if it is too painful, I understand." I said compassionately.

"It's okay man," Ra adds. "It's okay"

Kerry bows his head. Then raises it up quickly as though a spirit of light just hit him.

"The night before she was sold off Lila and I talked about so much. It's like I know everything that we talked about in my heart, but I can't put it in to words. She was so beautiful lying on top of me both her arms were folded on top of each other placed between my chest and her chin. She seemed so woman-ly, yet so child-like. We said how much we loved each other over and over again. I didn't know why I was saying it so sincerely. I mean….I knew I meant it. There was no doubt, from the moment I saw her she captivated me beyond words and feelings. Those nights although I was tired and worn out she rubbed my aching muscles, help the kids with their baths, and made something to eat out of the scraps Rev and Kat brought from the big house. When she cuddled next to me we spoke about the kids and the people in the village. From that Saturday night until Thursday her last words were "I love you husband, and I thank God for you and my family." That touched me beyond anything any woman has ever said to me."

"That last night she told me that she had a dream the previous night. She dreamt a beautiful angel came and took us along with the kids to a far away place in the stars. There I saw no whites, she said. All the Africans talked the way that you, John and some of the others have been talking since Raylene's funeral. She said that we had a special place of our own. The kids played under a clear cool waterfall, while I sat on the grass playing a drum looking at her dance like the ancestors. There were elders present who laughed and smile."

"When Lila was telling me this dream it was as if we were one. I could see everything that she was saying; I had such a warm feeling. She remained on top of me. As we began to make love, I could see a stream of tears coming out of her eyes against the flickering of the light that came from the quaint little fire that was burning in the corner. There was an old wool cover that served as a petition between the kids and us. I didn't feel embarrassed if they saw or heard us; it was so natural and wholesome. This kind of lovemaking was none like I ever experienced. She had her hands placed on both sides of my face, leaning forward and kissing me every so often very slowly, reassuring me how much she wanted to be close and to please me. She never once closed her eyes, staring at me with a warm smile; occasionally she'd wipe back a tear. When I began to reach climax, she never let me hurry; she was in control of my anxiety by placing her hands in my chest. I tried to rise up and capture the energy that was flowing. She slowed down barely moving. I never reached a climax like that before. As I looked through my eyelids for a moment, I could see her eyes barely open. Her smile widen as the tears had stopped streaming down her face. I had never come with any woman. I don't remember anything else after that. The next morning I awoke with Lila still on my chest, the kids were standing there laughing at us. She shooed them away as we turned to each other and laughed. At that moment I knew I would be all right if we didn't make it back."

I was amazed at Kerry's story. The gang was mesmerized as well. Katherine and Lizzy were both crying at what they considered the greatest love story ever told. Kerry too had watery eyes.

"I had to ask huh?" I said.

"I guess you knew I had to say it."

The ladies got up and hugged Kerry, then the fellas. Rev got up last and told Kerry to hold on to his dreams.

"Last but not least," I said. You ready preacher-man?"

"Let's do it!" replied Rev enthusiastically. I gave him his que.

"Well, I promised to keep this as short as possible."

"Yeah right," say Aaron breaking the mood brought on by Kerry's story.

"Getting to my story," Rev said easily.

"I've really been praying and meditating on this whole thing. I read the book "The History of the Council of Nicea" about the Roman Emperor Constantine and how he summoned nearly all the bishops and priests in various provinces and countries. How he waged this life or death campaign to tamper and change the order and implement new things in accordance with the Greco-Roman culture, a campaign that produce, for lack of a better term, a universal religion that mimicked a new world order that is what Catholicism means in Latin. It told what changes he made in accordance with tithing and taxing which was so preposterous that some bishops were exiled for refusing to follow. A few were even killed because they could not go along with the changes that were proposed and made."

"I believe that the Bible is still "the book" and a majority of people don't disagree, but they probably would if I told them that it teaches one thing, yet it is preached from another area and I know that area very well. I have studied time and time again. It is an area that we understood fairly well before we were put on any slave ship four hundred years ago. It was a spiritual system that began in the Nile Valley region thousands of years ago. There was nothing wrong with what we had when we got on the slave ship, but it was terrible for the slave owner. He knew in order to continue to keep dominion and rule over us he had to get rid of our spiritual system, and he did. He replaced it with teaching his version of the Bible, which stems from an African system, yet refurbished and changed in it's application or better still, it's preaching.

"The African knew that he was not disconnected from God and nature. As an agrarian (agriculture) society they knew it would be foolish to think God was outside of themselves; to them nature was also divine because it represented a reciprocal principle of the Creator. They applied this to life as well and out of this they began a spiritual system of divine life and death. Basically when a plant grows from a strong root and nurtured properly it bears food and dies, yet only to return in its cycle or seasonal time. Thus, ancestral worship was born. It is a magnificent honor to be an elder in an African society. It is divine to be an ancestor although there is much to learn in this area."

"The next time you go to your parent's home, or just dwell in yours, look at the pictures of those that have gone before you. Remember the things that your grandparents, aunts, uncles, moms and dads, or brothers, cousins and sisters and even husbands and wives left behind that you hold on to. It could be buttons, jewelry, clothing, tools, whatnots, etc. Get all these things together and put them on a table with some pictures. You now have a shrine to your ancestors. Talk to them. You do it anyway when you go visit their gravesite and place flowers on it. Don't you pray over it? It's all the same. You are more African than you would like to think and so is the Bible."

"What was the defining point for you on the journey?" I asked.

"Ressie!" replied Rev with no hesitation.

"She was wise and intuitive beyond words." The gang nodded their heads in agreement.

"She reminded me who and what God really is and how I was perpetrating somewhat of a fraud. I denied any direct intention to promote my own agenda, but any position of authority especially the clergy cannot be a victim to the overwhelming response of respect from the people. Ressie gave me a good ol' tongue lashing on manhood and God consciousness. Believe it or not, most of us feel that way, but don't teach in that fashion for fear of retaliation from councils, but there is no way I will stand in any pulpit and not express and teach the Creator's true expectations from its people and with that, I say Ashe'-Amen."

I said, "Ashe-Amen." Reaching out to turn off my tape I surveyed the room and the faces of the gang.

"That's quite an experience. I don't know what it is that's in me, but it sure does make me wanna believe it. There's too much sincerity and pain in all of this, too many lessons for people, such as us to just get together and fabricate the whole thing. So with some editing, I don't see any reason why this story should not make it to print."

"Well Ra! Are there any last words before I go? Is there anything different you plan on doing at the center or are you just gonna let these good folks here make your job a lot easier?"

"There is one area I plan to concentrate on more Horus, and that's reading. "There were so many lessons learned on that journey that we could be here all night telling one after the other. There are, however, two important lessons that I know will stay with me forever. The first one is to put more emphasis on reading; looking back at brother Zeke, I think we all realized that even though we were worlds apart, all he ever wanted was to learn how to read. Aside from us being black and enslaved all this brother ever wanted was to elevate himself enough by reading so he could be whatever man he wanted to become. Also, he wanted to please his woman. He simply just wanted to read. No money involved, no promotions, it wasn't a competitive or a one up- man-ship kind of thing, but Zeke knew that there was power in knowing how to read. With reading his spirit would then teach him to study the words. He would gain knowledge and information and then matters would grow. The consciousness of his environment would be exposed. Zeke knew that if he would ever be caught, his life would probably be on the line, and it was. However, it never mattered to him. His friendship with Aaron was based on two African brothers helping each other, one teaching the other how to read, and the other teaching the value of learning how to teach. Nowadays you can barely pay any African American to read. Its concept has been taken so much for granted. Students in classrooms across the country are still illiterate like many slaves and I bet if you follow them, most have parents at home who are worse. After all, that's what our elders went through in the fifties and sixties fighting for Civil Rights. The least we could do is pick up something that concerns our history, our people and our future. Looking back at what Zeke went through to learn how to read is probably the one thing that will always stay in my mind when I see a school student. I wish they all could, parents included see what we did. Seeing that brother being beaten that way will forever be in our minds; those sounds he made seemed almost inhuman." Ra slowly shakes his head.

"And the second lesson my friend?" I asked.

"This is probably the hardest thing for any African in America that is truly consciously aware is to know who the real enemies in our environment are. It is us! An elder once said to me that the biggest racists toward Black people are Black people. We hurt, despise and hate ourselves so much it leads to abandonment, violence and even murder. In all this so-called conspiracy by the White people to kill us, we had not stop to see that the majority of Black folks are getting killed by Black folk. And if they have planted the seed of death in our community then we need to dig it up and destroy it before it grows. We must become patient, under-standing, tolerant, and accepting of the fellow Africans in America who don't know, don't care to know, and even more sadly will ridicule and mock those who do know something of their history, culture and are striving to become educated in self-awareness. I know I have to accept these brothers and sisters as individuals who for whatever reason, it's just ain't their time to understand anything that's affiliated with being conscious. They literally despise the word 'Africa' itself. They are embarrassed by it and can't understand why anyone else would want to be affiliated with it and everything about it. That is why you see the speech that I have framed on my wall from brother Malcom on Africa and Self-hate."

I stood and walked over to the wall eyeing the words of Malcom X.

"Read it out Horus" says Rev.

"Yeah I like to hear what that fine brother has said on the matter," Lizzy adds.

AFRICA AND SELF-HATE

Now what effect does [the struggle over Africa] have on us? Why should the black man in America concern himself since he's been away from the African continent for three or four hundred years? Why should we concern our-selves? What impact does what happens to them have upon us? Number one, you have to realize that up until 1959 Africa was dominated by the colonial powers. Having complete con-trol over Africa, the colonial powers of Europe projected the image of Africa negatively. They always project Africa in a negative light: jungle savages, cannibals, nothing civilized. Why then naturally it was so negative that it was negative to you and me, and you and I began to hate it. We didn't want anybody telling us anything about Africa, much less calling us Africans. In hating Africa and in hating the Africans, we ended up hating ourselves, without even real-izing it. Because you can't hate the roots of a tree, and not hate the tree. You can't hate your origin and not end up hating yourself. You can't hate Africa and not hate yourself.

You show me one of these people over here who has been thoroughly brainwashed and has a negative attitude toward Africa, and I'll show you one who has a negative attitude toward himself. You can't have a positive attitude toward yourself and a negative attitude toward Africa at the same time. To the same degree that your understanding of and attitude toward Africa become positive, you'll find that your understanding of and your attitude toward yourself will also become positive. And this is what the white man knows. So they very skillfully make you and me hate our African identity, our African characteristics.

You know yourself that we have been a people who hated our African characteristics. We hated our heads, we hated the shape of our nose, we wanted one of those long noses, you know; we hated the color of our skin, hated the blood of Africa that was in our veins. And in hating our features and our skin and our blood, why, we had to end up hating ourselves. And we hated ourselves. Our color became to us a chain – we felt that it was holding us back; our color became to us like a prison which we felt was keeping us confined, not letting us go this way or that way. We felt that all of these restrictions were based solely upon our color, and the psychological reaction to that would have to be that as long as we felt imprisoned or chained or trapped by black skin, black features and black blood, that skin and those features and that blood holding us back automatically had to become hateful to us. And it became hateful to us.

It made us feel inferior; it made us feel inadequate; made us feel helpless. And when we fell victims to this feeling of inadequacy or inferiority or helplessness, we turned to somebody else to show us the way. We didn't have confidence in another black man to show us the way, or black people to show us the way. In those days we didn't. We didn't think a black man could do anything except play some horns – you know, make some sound and make you happy with some songs and in that way. But in serious things, where our food, clothing, shelter and education were concerned, we turned to the man. We never thought in terms of bringing these things into existence for ourselves, we never thought in terms of doing things for ourselves. Because we felt helpless. What made us feel helpless was our hatred for ourselves. And our hatred for ourselves stemmed from our hatred for things African . . .

(Malcolm X Speaks)

I ended the speech. "I believe that this speech will be the final word on this interview and my article. I bid you all a farewell. I leave knowing that the African American community and the city of Buffalo Hill will be a much better place to live."

The gang rose and exchanged farewell hugs. They know they are family and that the connection is rooted in their ancestry. They are their ancestors and their existence on this day, at this time, in this place, is because those Africans were. "Ashe! Hotep!"

ABOUT THE AUTHOR

Stephen Mackey is a native Houstonian, the father of four boys and a former Sunday school teacher. He carries a degree in both education and political science. A former international athlete, he established himself both in Europe and S. America as an exceptional basketball player. Mr. Mackey retired from Corporate America as a manager in 2004.

Before and after his retirement, Mackey a child of the 60's with a first hand perspective on the civil rights movement and other church and community based struggles of Black Americans was always thirsty for more knowledge about the true heritage and culture of African peoples. With a strong experiential understanding of the necessity and rewards of struggle, perseverance and seeking knowledge, he became more involved in inner city grass roots organizations and communities of African Americans in Houston, Mackey intensified his studies into the culture of Africans both here and on the Continent under the instructions of Dr. Afolabi Epega,. His exposure to other local and national historians positioned him to utilize his natural gift for communicating and translating information from the academicians to the everyday neighborhood folk. It was inevitable that he would become one of the most dynamic teachers on African history and spirituality in the Houston area.

Traveling regularly to Africa over the past few years, Mackey was initiated as a Priest in the West African spiritual system of Ifa. These along with his other talents and experiences have established him on both the east and west coasts as a trusted Life Coach and spiritual counselor.

RECOMMENDED READINGS

Dr. Afolabi A. Epega. <u>IFA The Ancient Wisdom</u> Athelia Henrietta Press, Brooklyn, NY., 2003

Malidoma Patrice Some. <u>Of Water and Spirit Ritual, Magic and Initiation in the Life of an African Shaman</u> Penguin (Non-Classics); New York, N.Y., Reprint edition (May 1, 1995)

Malidoma Patrice Some. <u>Healing Wisdom of Africa.</u> Penguin Putnam, New York, N.Y. 1998

Anthony Browder. <u>Nile Valley Contributions to Civilization.</u> Institute of Karmic Guidance, Washington, D.C., 1992

Chancellor Williams. <u>Destruction of Black Civilization.</u> Third World Press, Chicago, Ill., 1987

Helen Ellerbe. <u>The Dark Side of Christian History</u>. Morning & Lark, Orlando, FL., 1995